PENNSYLVANIA FIRESIDE TALES

VOLUME 7

JEFFREY R. FRAZIER

CATAMOUNT
PRESS

an imprint of Sunbury Press, Inc.
Mechanicsburg, PA USA

CATAMOUNT
PRESS

an imprint of Sunbury Press, Inc.
Mechanicsburg, PA USA

For information about special discounts for bulk purchases, please contact Sunbury Press
Orders Dept. at (855) 338-8359 or orders@sunburypress.com.

To request one of our authors for speaking engagements or book signings, please contact
Sunbury Press Publicity Dept. at publicity@sunburypress.com.

FIRST CATAMOUNT PRESS EDITION: January 2025

Set in Adobe Garamond | Interior design by Crystal Devine | Cover by Lawrence Knorr | Edited by Debra
Reynolds.

Publisher's Cataloging-in-Publication Data
Names: Frazier, Jeffrey R., author.
Title: Pennsylvania fireside tales volume 7 / Jeffrey R. Frazier.
Description: First trade paperback edition. | Mechanicsburg, PA : Catamount Press, 2025.
Summary: Volume 7 in the Pennsylvania Fireside Tales series exploring the origins and foundations of
old-time Pennsylvania mountain folktales, legends, and folklore.
Identifiers: ISBN : 979-8-88819-260-3 (paperback).
Subjects: NATURE / Ecosystems & Habitats / Mountains | HISTORY / United States / State & Local /
Middle Atlantic (DC, DE, MD, NJ, NY, PA) | FICTION / Fairy Tales, Folk Tales & Mythology.

Designed in the USA
0 1 1 2 3 5 8 13 21 34 55

For the Love of Books!

Cover: Based on a crop of *The Lackawanna Valley*, c. 1856 by George Inness, displayed at the National Galley of Art in
Washington, DC.

Indians at the Wyoming Massacre. Print from Scribner's Magazine (New York: Chas. Scribner's & Sons, 1887) entitled "The Indians departing after the massacre of Wyoming." Creator: Frederick Coffay Yohn. "Picture Collection, the Branch Libraries, The New York Public Library, Astor, Lenox and Tilden Foundations, #833783." See the chapter titled "Queen Esther's Rock" for a related story about the terrible events that occurred here.

CONTENTS

In winter's tedious nights sit by the fire
With good old folks, and let them tell their tales
Of woeful ages long ago betide

—Shakespeare
Tragedy of Richard II

INTRODUCTION

This is a book I had not planned to write. When I started my *Pennsylvania Fireside Tales* series, I thought it would end up as a set of six unique volumes. In fact, on the front cover of *Volume VI* I noted that it was, indeed, the last volume of the series. However, I didn't feel quite right about it. I still had some colorful tales left that I wanted to share with readers but didn't think that there were quite enough to fill yet another volume.

Fate, on the other hand, seemed to have other ideas. After *Volume VI* was published in 2005 I continued to get invitations to speak in front of various groups, which I've always enjoyed immensely. My talk, which I title "Pennsylvania Mountain Folktales and Legends—Fact or Fancy," has always been well received, and inevitably when I end my presentation someone always comes up and shares a tale with me that they feel might deserve inclusion in my next book.

As a result of these pleasant interchanges, I acquired some anecdotes over the last two years that include some of the best material I've found in my thirty-seven years of collecting the state's folktales, legends, and oral history. These new additions to my treasure chest of tales led me to decide that a seventh volume was definitely possible and certainly necessary, not only to preserve these new additions for posterity but also to preserve the other colorful tales I had left to share.

Another benefit of producing a seventh volume is that I would have an opportunity to expand on previous tales for which I had collected additional facts since they were first published. One of the best examples of a situation like that relates to a tale in my *Volume II* called "The Lower Fort" in which I describe a frontier massacre that occurred near the frontier fort called Potter's Fort, in Potter Township of Centre County in 1778.

A number of years after that volume was published, I was put in touch with the great-great-great-great grandson of the young Standford boy who was captured by warriors during that raid, and who later escaped. Abraham Standford's descriptions of his time on the frontier were preserved by his descendants and they are such gems of unsurpassed value that they should not be lost. For that reason, they are included in the story in this volume entitled "War Whoop and Scalping Knife."

Consequently, as a result of my good fortune in finding the new tales and in having some of equal quality left from previous years of collecting, readers will now have an opportunity to enjoy them all, including one which local folks have asked me about in the past since it was never included in the first six volumes. This old account, the tale of the Ingleby Monster, has grabbed the attention of young folks in my region for at least fifty to one-hundred years, and it still circulates today.

The hair-raising anecdote, which can be found in the present volume's chapter titled "Dark Side of the Mountains," captures the imagination because of its bone-chilling details but also because the place where it is said to have occurred is, even yet today, so isolated and wild; two factors which inevitably cause people to wonder if what the story relates just might be true.

Similar to many of the other tales in my books that seem to be of the far-fetched variety, there is good reason to argue that they never really happened; that they are instead just colorful creations from the minds of good storytellers. However, even though my objective in each of my books has been to explore whether or not the stories included therein have any basis in fact, I've always found, regardless of what might be concluded about a tale's origins, that they do cause us to pause and wonder. And in that way, if nothing else, they make life a little more fascinating and entertaining.

If that is one of the legacies I leave behind with my books, to have entertained some folks over time, then it will have been worth the effort. Then too, if the books instill in people a greater appreciation for Pennsylvania's mountains and wild areas, thereby deterring a would-be litterbug or saving ten acres of mountain or forest land from the advance of so-called progress, then they will have served a good purpose in this regard as well.

Certainly, I would have liked to have done better and done more, but that was not possible when doing this as a hobby. I've never tried to present myself as a historian, folklorist, or some other trained person who was more professionally qualified to take on the task I've pursued since 1970, but I have tried to be as thorough as possible in my investigations. In fact, as close as anyone could come to assigning a label to me was a young gentleman who, upon hearing what I was doing and how I tried to delve into the origins of the tales I was collecting, commented, "Oh, so you're an investigative reporter?"

At first, I thought he had nailed it, but then I realized that even investigative reporters should verify all their facts and establish the reliability of all their sources before publishing a story. Obviously in the realm of folktales and legends you can only go so far along those investigative paths, and if I had assiduously adhered to that credo then there never would have even been a first volume in this series, let alone six others besides.

So I guess the legacy I leave behind is a set of books containing lots of colorful and entertaining anecdotes that readers will have to evaluate for themselves as far as whether or not the tales are grounded in truth in any way. On the other hand, if there is any truth to comments I've gotten from readers in the past, the tales will, if nothing else, inspire you to go out into the Pennsylvania hills and visit the spots where the events described in the stories themselves are said to have occurred. If so, then the books will have provided yet another source of enjoyment for those who are inspired to journey off the beaten path and into the less-traveled back roads of the Keystone State.

And with respect to those back roads, I have acquired a few more favorite stories and mountain vistas during my picture-taking and story-collecting trips over the last two years. The vistas are in addition to those overlooks mentioned in my last volumes, and all are prospects that rival in beauty many of those that can be found in more famous spots like Great Smoky Mountains National Park or the Blue Ridge Mountains of Tennessee and Virginia. So, I will leave you with these three for your further viewing pleasure; all are worth a trip:

- Kettle Road, along Broad Mountain in Huntingdon County. This rough gravel road passes by Milligan's Knob in Rothrock State Forest. At 2,320 feet the peak is the highest mountain in the Seven Mountains country.

- Route 44 along White Deer Ridge in Lycoming County. Unsurpassed views can be seen between the villages of Collomsville and Elimsport.

- Route 164 in the Allegheny Mountains of Blair and Cambria Counties. Views between the villages of Smith Corner (Blair) and Martindale (Cambria) are exceptional and as close to anything I've seen in the Blue Ridge Mountains of North Carolina.

A word or two about the last chapter in this volume also would seem appropriate at this point. It includes stories from some of the old-time airmail pilots who flew the open cockpit biplanes in the infancy of the United States Airmail Service. Although all other episodes in my books have much earlier roots, these tales take us into the modern age, and therefore seem to be a fitting conclusion to what I think this time is really the last book in the *Pennsylvania Fireside Tales* series.

AUTHOR'S NOTE

The preceding paragraphs are what appeared in the first edition of this volume, and the chapters that appear in this edition are the same ones that were included in all previous ones. There are also two new chapters in this new Sunbury Press edition that did not appear in any of the previous ones, and there are also additions to the original chapters. These extras include interesting details that were discovered after the last edition was published and which I felt needed to be added to the chapters in order to enhance their quality. This new Sunbury Press edition also has many new photos not included in previous editions, but which add a whole new level of interest to the original tales. I hope these enhancements add to the reader's enjoyment.

CHAPTER I

PANTHER DAYS
(AND NIGHTS)

Lehigh County was once a treasure trove of old-time Pennsylvania legends and folktales, but over the years almost all have been forgotten—lost in the currents of time. However, there was one legend here that proved to have a longer lifespan than any others in the area; longevity attributable, no doubt, to the macabre nature of the tale. As a matter of fact, for over 150 years the account cast a shadow of fear over the sacred ground of a little country church in the lower part of that same county.

That's not surprising, however, considering the fact that the episode was described in one early account as "a story of horror, gloom, and death."[1] Said to date back to the late 1700s, the old tale could still be heard along the foothills of the Blue Mountains as late as the mid-1940s, and it is said that it was often responsible for causing even some of the area's bravest men to walk a little faster when passing by the graveyard where the events related in the legend supposedly occurred.

The Salisbury Church and its graveyard still can be found on a hillside north of Emmaus, Lehigh County, but it's no longer the isolated spot it once was in the 1700s. Back then this "church in the wildwood" appeared normal during the day, but at night it was said to take on a gloomy and sinister appearance to those who knew its legend. And that legend told of a local miscreant who had sold his soul to Satan in order to save his life when fighting in the Revolutionary War.

---

1. Thomas R. Brendle and William S Troxell, "Pennsylvania German Folk Tales, Legends, Once-upon-a-time Stories, Maxims, and Sayings," *Proceedings of the Pennsylvania German Society, Volume L*, 68.

It was an effective insurance policy. The man came through the war physically unscathed, but it became a matter of debate as to the state of his mental faculties when he returned home. His cronies at the bar he frequented would often hear him boast that now that he was back, his first order of business would be to "lay low" another local man against whom he held a deep-seated grudge.

Those of sound minds knew that the boast was a futile one; the man's hated enemy now lay buried in the churchyard on the hill. Nonetheless, the veteran of bloody engagements with the King's redcoats swore that his "cowardly" foe could not even hide from him in his grave, and that he knew of a way to bring him out to fight. Then one night, after many rounds of hard liquor in the local tavern, the ruffian made that same boast again, and his drinking companions, most of whom were as drunk as the boaster, dared him to confront his rival that very evening.

With a string of oaths, the would-be antagonist stormed out of the tavern while calling forth his enemy from the bowels of the earth. The same summons was heard once more when the drunken man reached the cemetery gate, but then shrill screams and wild cries floated down to the listeners in the tavern below, all of whom, to a man, had not had the courage to go along to view the ungodly combat that was to take place.

Truth be told, there was also not a single tavern patron who could summon up enough courage to go up the hill that night to see what might have happened to their friend, and it wasn't until the next morning that a few of the braver individuals found his mangled body, bloody and naked, lying in the graveyard.

Those of a more superstitious frame of mind believed that the war veteran had actually been killed by the fiendish spirit of the man he had summoned forth from the grave, but others said that there was a more mundane explanation. These free thinkers noted that the man merely picked the wrong time and place to be in the city of the dead that dark and foreboding night.

They contended that a panther had wandered into the graveyard before the man got there, thinking it could sleep here undisturbed, but when the drunken intruder interrupted its rest, the big cat attacked and mangled him. However, no matter which explanation was espoused, everyone was

An old time hunter. Luther Weaver of Woodward, Centre County, showing off his many trophies of the chase, may have been more than a match for any panther (photo courtesy of Vonnie Henninger.)

convinced that the matter was an act of God, and divine justice had been duly meted out.[2]

The Lehigh County legend does not say whether locals finally solved the mysterious murder at the Salisbury Church graveyard, but the old tale does serve as a good starting point for relating some real panther encounters that actually occurred in the Pennsylvania hills over the last two hundred years.

Unlike the Lehigh County tale, it can be easily accepted that the events preserved in the following episodes actually happened and portray a time in Pennsylvania's past that was—and may be becoming so again—a period where danger lurked in the tall trees and dark hollows of Penn's Woods. Certainly one old Centre County couple, if they were alive yet today, would agree that panthers were once a force to be reckoned with in the mountains of Keystone State.

John and Lucretia DeLong lived in a log cabin in the mountains near Livonia, Centre County, during the decades immediately preceding the Civil War. There are a number of different mountains that surround the little town that used to be a Mecca for hunters of the state's big game animals,

---

2. Ibid.

Site of the old watering trough. Local tales say that it was here, along present-day Route 305, on Stone Mountain, Huntingdon County, that an old-time country doctor and his thirsty horse were attacked by a large panther around 1900.

and it's not known for sure today on which peak the rustic dwelling that John fashioned with his own hands stood.

However, regardless of whether it was on Nittany, Hough, Brush, or Hall Mountain, or even on Sugar Valley Mountain to the north, it is agreed by the DeLongs' descendants that their ancestors lived in a home that was located in a lonely and wild place in those days; one they shared with both wolves and mountain lions.

Born in 1792 in Nazareth, Pennsylvania, city boy John DeLong was not afraid of a life on the frontier, nor was his wife, Lucretia. She was not quite thirty years old when, around 1848, she and her mate moved on to the mountains above present-day Livonia.

Mrs. DeLong worked as hard as her husband to make the place their home. Despite the nightly screams and howls of wild beasts, and the sense of danger those sounds evoked, John and Lucretia actually found the area to be a spot they enjoyed—as witnessed by the name they assigned to their alpine retreat. They called it Mount Pleasant. However, things were not always pleasant for the DeLongs when they lived at Mount Pleasant, particularly on that frightening day when a panther decided to hitch a ride on their topped buggy.

The DeLongs' descendants don't know where John and Lucretia were headed on that particular day, but wherever it was, they took their horse and buggy. The buggy had a canvas top over it to protect its riders from snow and rain, but the sides were open for easy entrance and exit, much like topped Amish buggies today.

On most trips it must have been a pleasant experience to ride through the mountains in the conveyance, since its top afforded some protection from the elements, while the open sides allowed its passengers to smell the fragrances of the deep woods and enjoy the cool breezes of the forest. Those delights were fleeting on this trip, as the DeLongs' enjoyment of their natural surroundings was short-lived and rudely interrupted.

At some point on their journey, probably at one of the most secluded and heavily wooded areas on the mountain, the DeLongs' reveries were jarred by the sound of something that landed on the canvas overhead. They must have realized it was a heavy object from the noise it made, but they most likely didn't realize it was a big cat until it screamed and began clawing at the canvas top.

What Mrs. Delong's exact reaction might have been is not recalled by family members today anymore, but she no doubt screamed, and hollered for her husband to do something. There was not much he could do since he apparently did not have his gun along with him, but he knew that some immediate action was needed in order to save their lives.

What he did next will probably sound far-fetched to many folks today, but perhaps many of us would have made the same move in the same situation. John DeLong's quick-thinking reaction, according to DeLong descendants, was to grab his buggy whip.

By that time the horse had no doubt bolted, frightened out of its wits by the panther on the buggy roof directly behind it. DeLong probably knew he couldn't stop the terrified horse, and he certainly hadn't grabbed the buggy whip with the intention of using it in the normal way—that is, cracking it to speed the horse up. There was no use in trying to run away, and since flight was not an option, DeLong knew he had to fight, and that's exactly what he did.

Leaning out the side of the buggy, the steely mountaineer drew back his arm and then began flailing the mountain cat with the whip. The attack must have surprised the formidable creature; it was a defense it had never seen before, and it was not sure how to manage it.

Perhaps it clawed at the whip a time or two, and most probably growled at it as well, but finally the panther jumped off the buggy roof and bounded back into the thick woods, where it must have decided that there were easier pickings somewhere else. As for the DeLongs, they probably agreed that they had traveled far enough that day. They also may have also concluded that the next time they took a buggy ride, a gun might be a good traveling companion.[3]

Guns, however, proved to be of no use to two men who encountered panthers, back in the first decade of the twentieth century near the small village of McAlevys Fort in Huntingdon County's Stone Valley. Typical of panther stories that were once common throughout the state, these two stirring tales are also interesting because of the way the big cats managed to cheat death. In one case the panther got away because his intended victim decided not to shoot it after all, and in the second case the cat had what seemed to be a sixth sense that kept it safe from a hunter's bullet.

Both tales come down to us today from old-time lumberman Thomas Milton Wilson who was born near McAlevys Fort in 1885. In his last years, the rough and ready mountaineer delighted in recalling these episodes to his grandchildren, who were lucky enough to have him still around when they were old enough to appreciate his tales of an earlier and simpler time.

Today those same grandchildren are happy to pass his stories on to others who are usually as delighted to hear them as the old man was in telling them. Two of his favorites were panther tales—one being of a personal encounter on Broad Mountain, and the other about another man who lost his horse but not his life when attacked by a big mountain lion on Stone Mountain.

Wilson's personal encounter with a Pennsylvania mountain lion occurred around 1900, about the same time that the heavy timbering conducted by lumber companies all over the state had finally destroyed most of the natural cover and food supplies that deer depended upon to survive.

---

3. Kay McFate, interviewed June 12, 2005.

Left: John DeLong. When a panther jumped onto their topped buggy, John resorted to a unique way of saving his life, and that of his wife, by chasing the beast away in a bold and dangerous way that most of us would find unbelievable today. Right: Lucretia DeLong. Wife of John DeLong who was riding with him when a panther jumped onto their topped buggy. (Photos courtesy of Kathryn McFate.)

This unchecked destruction of natural resources had reduced the state's deer herd to a few scrawny stragglers, and so whenever a hunter spotted a deer track in those times it was a pleasant surprise. It was also enough incentive to cause most hunters of that era to grab their guns and follow the tracks. Wilson was no exception.

A light skiff of snow lay on the ground one fall morning when Wilson walked into the woods to work at his family's lumber mill near McAlevys Fort. As the teenager made his way through the foothills of Broad Mountain he kept his eyes on the ground, looking for telltale signs of wild game. Then he saw the unmistakable tracks in the light snow. He had stumbled across, or in the words of the seasoned hunter, "cut" a deer trail. All thoughts of work immediately went out of his mind, and the young man turned around and went back to his parent's house for his gun.

After picking up his weapon and packing some food to take along, young Wilson set off on what he hoped would be a short trek. He was determined to follow the deer as long as necessary to bring it down, but by the time the noon hour arrived without his even catching sight of his quarry, he could have been excused for thinking that he may have bitten off more than he could chew.

Thinking that the deer might settle into a spot to feed as nighttime approached, and that he therefore might have a better chance of coming up on it later in the day, the young hunter decided to take a short nap and continue his quest at night.

It was late afternoon when he found a leafy bed in a hollow spot on the forest floor, and he soon dozed off. He had just fallen into a light slumber when he was awakened by the sensation that someone was throwing leaves onto his face. The unexpected feeling caused his eyes to snap open, and then it did not take him long to realize the terrible predicament he was in.

Much to his dismay, he could see a large panther busily using its rear feet to scatter fallen leaves on top of him. He knew that the panther thought he was dead and therefore a potential meal. He also knew that any movement on his part would provoke an attack, and so he lay as still as he could until he was completely covered. The mountain lion then turned and walked away, as though tired of its little game.

After the big cat had disappeared, the frightened young man got up from his leafy grave, and with gun in hand, scrambled up the highest and sturdiest tree he could find close by. The tree was a safer spot than being on the ground, and Wilson also figured he could see the panther better from a loftier perch if the big predator came back to look for him.

He did not have long to wait before the large cat returned, slinking quietly through the woods and then creeping slowly up to the pile of leaves. Finally, when it was close enough, the ferocious animal pounced upon the leafy mound, thinking its sleeping prey was still there.

At that point, the fearless boy in the tree raised his rifle and drew a bead on the animal that had intended to kill him. However, just as he was about to pull the trigger, he noticed that the lioness had two small cubs with her. She must have brought them along for what she thought would be an easy meal or even an easy lesson in stalking and killing prey for her cubs, but her intentions had been somehow thwarted and now she would have to make a kill somewhere else that day if her cubs were not to go hungry.

Perhaps sensing the animal's frustration and despair, the treed rifleman decided he "didn't have the heart," as he would later say, to shoot the cubs' mother. He knew he was out in the woods far enough that the hungry panther would not be a threat to any livestock back home, and so he decided not to gun her down. Perhaps he had second thoughts as he watched the glowing eyes of the mother and her cubs disappear into the darkening forest, but he stuck with his decision to spare the hungry lioness' life so she could provide for her litter and see them grow to adulthood.[4]

Tom Wilson's account is regarded as factual by his descendants since he is remembered by them as a "no-nonsense kind of guy" who wasn't prone to telling tall tales. Moreover, the part of his story about the panther covering him with leaves is corroborated by none other than Sam Askey, the great Pennsylvania panther hunter of the Alleghenies.

In relating an incident where he shot and killed a panther that was about to attack him because he got too close to a carcass of a deer "covered with leaves" that the beast was guarding, Askey told his biographer that "venison is a panther's choice meat, and when he kills one and has satisfied his appetite, he covers the carcass and lays near, taking his meals regularly until all of it is consumed."[5]

Actually being covered with leaves by a panther was a far more serious brush with death than a similar encounter Wilson had one night about ten years later, when he was coming back across Broad Mountain after spending a pleasant evening courting his future wife. The smitten beau had stayed later than usual at Nanny May Henninger's home that night, and to make matters worse he had forgotten to fill his lantern with kerosene before heading back through the darkening forest.

He had not gotten too far before the lantern began to sputter and its light died out completely. Fortunately, the sky was clear, and the moon was full that night, and so there was just enough moonlight to guide him along his way. For the lone traveler it was light enough that it didn't take long for his eyes to adjust to the point where they could begin to discern objects in the soft white glow that permeated the woods.

Straining to keep his eyes on the path so as not to lose his way, Wilson suddenly spotted what looked to be an animal coming toward him on the trail ahead. Perhaps his imagination got the best of him, but the more he

4. Dan Wilson (born 1951), recorded November 17, 2005.
5. John Blair Linn, *History of Centre and Clinton Counties*, 422.

View of the Salisbury church graveyard. Largely remaining the way it looked a hundred years ago the old resting place, interestingly enough, still holds the remains of many Revolutionary War veterans, and even of Indians who once called the area their home. Their stories lend a macabre atmosphere to this remote spot.

looked at the creature in front of him the more he became convinced that it had to be the panther that many folks had recently reported seeing in the area and which had killed one of his neighbor's hogs.

At this point he stopped dead in his tracks and decided not to move any further, and the animal, seemingly deciding upon the same strategy, stopped as well. There the two nocturnal travelers stood, in a face-to-face standoff, until Wilson decided to force the issue.

The young lumberman had always enjoyed listening to the panther tales the old hunters in the area would tell of their younger hunting days, and from that local lore Wilson believed that mountain lions were not the fearsome beasts many folks believed them to be. After all, he had heard those who should know the facts firsthand say that the big cats would try to pounce on their prey, either from a tree or from a running start, but that if they missed their target or did not make a good hit on their first try, they would generally run away.

Upon recalling that fact, Wilson decided it was a sound enough basis for his next move, which, he felt, was the only thing he could do if he was going to survive this encounter. Slowly the lone wayfarer hunkered himself down until his chest rested upon his knees.

Then, once he felt his legs were ready to provide the most powerful spring he could get from them, the determined hiker, screaming and hollering as loud as he could, took a running dive at the beast on the trail. He had judged the distance well, hitting the animal with the impact he had hoped for.

However, when he did bump into the beast, it gave a loud yelp, turned, and fled into the night. Given his leafy experience of some ten years earlier, it's easy to imagine the young man's relief as watched his neighbor's dog run away with its tail between its legs, howling in fear.

Wilson later decided that the dog had been so scared by his actions that, judging from the way it ran away from him, it must have run all the way back to its home at top speed, never slowing down once, neither to catch its breath nor to see if the "panther" that had attacked it was still hot and heavy on its tail.[6]

Among the stories of real panther episodes passed on to Wilson by his elderly neighbors in Stone Valley was one account that told of another man whose luck was also with him one night when he was attacked by a large mountain lion along present-day Route 305 on Stone Mountain. The account shows once again not only how dedicated the doctors of that day and age actually were, but also how fearless and bold they sometimes had to be in order to perform their duties.

The tired country doctor had been summoned from his office in Belleville, Mifflin County, to deliver a baby at McAlevys Fort, Huntingdon County; and the trip had taken longer than he had planned. There was no trained medical practitioner in the little town named after the frontier blockhouse erected on the spot by Captain William McAlevy during the Revolutionary War, and so the Belleville physician was often called there to treat sick patients.

It was a long trip on horseback, and now on this late dark night there was hardly any moonlight by which to see. Then as the horse and rider approached that section of the road locals called Watering Trough Hill, the horse seemed to get "skittery."

6. Wilson, Ibid.

As they got closer to the old watering trough that sat along the sharpest bend in the road, the doctor sensed trouble. He had stopped here to allow his horse to drink many times before, but tonight the animal was acting funny and appeared to be frightened. With some effort, the horseman spurred his mount toward the liquid refreshment, but the darkness prevented him from seeing the mountain lion standing on the trough.

It was then that the huge cat made a leap at the horse and hit it with such force that it broke the animal's neck, causing both the animal and the doctor to fall down roughly onto the road. Although badly bruised and frightened, the physician managed to get up and run away.

The hungry cat was more interested in making a meal of the horse at that point, and so the fleeing doctor was able to make his escape. Unsure of what the panther might do next, he never stopped running until he saw the lights of the first farmhouse along the road. Here the winded man was able to get a gun and some help, and with these reinforcements went back to rescue his horse.

By the time the doctor got back to the place of the attack, his attacker was nowhere to be seen. It had disemboweled the horse and eaten a few mouthfuls of the entrails, but the panther's instincts had apparently warned it of the danger that was approaching.

Rather than take the risk of confronting that danger, the wily beast decided to forgo the rest of its hard-earned meal, slinking back into the deepest and darkest hollows of the mountains where it could enter its rocky den and go to sleep with a full stomach and without feeling the pangs of hunger.[7]

Whether or not the watering trough panther lived much longer after that is, of course, not known. Undoubtedly, a veritable army of hunters converged on the area after hearing of the good doctor's narrow escape. To a man they all were probably hoping to be the slayer of one of the last, if not the last, mountain lions in Stone Valley. Subsequently, one of those nimrods could very well have been successful in tracking down and killing the doctor's attacker.

At least the dates for the last panther bounties paid in Huntingdon and surrounding counties coincide with that time period. Unconfirmed reports indicate that the last Huntingdon County mountain lion bounty

---

7. Linn, Ibid.

was collected in 1911, and if that's true, that same lion might have been the beast that attacked the Huntingdon County doctor. If so, then it can be said that the lion finally paid the ultimate price for its boldness.

NOTE: As to whether it was large enough and strong enough to be able to knock over the doctor's horse and break its neck, there is some corroboration for that in an historical account describing how powerful the big cats could be.

In 1873, while hunters in the eastern hemlock forests of Potter County were busy hunting a lone wolf that was ravaging their flocks of sheep, they also were tracking a large panther which had also been killing sheep in that same section at a rate of fifteen sheep a night.

They knew it must be a large cat, having found a paw print measuring five inches in diameter. Moreover, they also found instances where tracks showed where the cat had pounced toward its prey and missed. In measuring the distance of several such jumps, they were surprised to find they ranged from "sixteen to twenty feet."[8]

---

8. J. H. Beers & Co., *History of McKean, Elk, Cameron, and Potter Counties Pennsylvania*, 1000.

CHAPTER 2

GHOSTS OF THE GRAVEYARD

Since the last chapter contained a story about a cemetery ghost, it seems fitting to continue in that "spirit" in this chapter.

It would no doubt be safe to say that almost any township in the state has its own haunted graveyard. Likewise, it might be noted that this writer has barely scratched the surface in gathering all such tales that could be collected if a serious effort were made to do so. Nonetheless, I think the following anecdotes will prove of interest to the reader. They are among the most unusual spook stories I've come across in my many years of collecting the state's legends and supernatural episodes, and I count them as some of my favorites.

Probably one of the least-visited graveyards in Pennsylvania is the old Rock Cemetery that sits on the grounds of Rockview State Penitentiary, near State College in Centre County. The prison once prohibited visitors from coming here, but in recent years access to it has been opened to the public. Nonetheless, it is doubtful whether anyone would want to go to this hallowed ground at the time the cemetery's ghost is supposed to appear.

Moreover, even if you went there at the appointed time and actually saw the ghost, people would no doubt accuse you of being "in your cups," as old-time mountain folks sometimes referred to anyone who has imbibed too freely. The reason for this possibility is because the time the ghost is said to materialize is at midnight on New Year's Eve.

Ghosts and graveyards are probably the last thing on the minds of revelers who like to usher in the New Year, but the weeping ghost of Rock

Statue of Augusta Bitner. Lancaster Cemetery, Lancaster County.

Cemetery, as I like to call her, if she exists, might appreciate the company of anyone who comes to her graveside on this particular night—a night known for its parties and for the hope and happiness the new year brings.

Since hope and happiness have eluded it for so long, the ghost might need reassurance that it will somehow experience those emotions once again. Visitors would perhaps breathe new energy into the lonely wraith, helping her materialize more often and in more discernible form.

What must be doubly troubling to the sad spirit is the fact that her tombstone is no longer standing; or has sunk into the earth so far that it is no longer evident that it was there in the first place. At least it was not visible when several of us went there in 1980 hoping to take a picture of

Closer View of Augusta Bitner's Statue.
Lancaster Cemetery, Lancaster County.

Face of the walking statue in
Lancaster Cemetery.

the old marker with its strange epitaph. Nor could we find it when arriving there at midnight on a New Year's in 2022.

Even if it was still there to be seen, it would not be hard to miss given the fact the inscription upon it is said to read "Died at Night." And it is this epitaph that serves as a reminder of the macabre legend that is associated with this forgotten and melancholy place.

The town of Rock was once a prosperous and vibrant community, growing up around General Philip Benner's Upper and Lower Rock iron forges, which he erected here in 1794 and 1800. The enterprising Revolutionary War veteran is said to have chosen the name for his little village from the rocky cliff-like ledges along the banks of nearby Spring Creek, which the General could view from his impressive stone mansion on the hill.

Although the cliffs are still there, the stately mansion, considered "an aristocratic affair for its day,"[1] was somewhat neglected after the General died, and eventually it fell into such a state of disrepair that it was razed altogether. Even all traces of the huge forges that were once prevalent landmarks here have been wiped out over time. Consequently, Rock is now just a place name, preserved, ironically enough, in the name of the state penitentiary that sits on lands once owned by Benner.

The only tangible reminder of the village of Rock left today is the cemetery where General Benner, his wife Ruth, and other former inhabitants of the little village were laid to rest. There is, however, according to the cemetery's old legend, one inhabitant of this sleeping city that cannot find that same rest and eternal peace.

Known as the Weeping Ghost, the unsettled spirit is said to be the remaining essence of a young lady who cannot entirely leave this earthly sphere until her body is given a proper burial. It seems that when she died, she was interred rather rapidly by the citizens of Rock, and if the legend is true, then they had good reason for doing so.

Apparently, the unfortunate woman's sister-in-law fell victim to a cholera scourge that spread rapidly through the area at some indefinite time in the past. However, neither time nor mercy were things the disease granted to its victims. Those who caught it died a horrible death due to the dehydration of the body brought about by the massive bouts of diarrhea caused by the illness. This young lady was no exception; and after she died, her

---

1. Linn, Ibid, 257.

relatives, including the young woman who was to become the so-called Weeping Ghost, came to her funeral to mourn her passing.

The good citizens of Rock were no doubt concerned that the pestilence would reach epidemic proportions. They apparently had no cure for the sickness, and so they knew they had to find ways to stop it from spreading. One of those ways, they must have concluded, was rapid burial of those who succumbed to the fatal malady.

And so it was, that when the deceased woman's sister-in-law, who apparently was dying from cholera as well, fainted dead away at the funeral, the horrified mourners left her where she had fallen and went back to their homes to construct a wooden coffin so they could bury her at once.

Supposedly it was dark by the time the burial party returned, and it is said that the interment was conducted in the midst of evening mists that swayed and moved uncertainly through the eerie shadows cast by lantern light. The circumstances of the young woman's passing, and the unearthly nocturnal atmosphere, made it a mission that all those in the funeral party wanted to be done with as soon as possible. Consequently, once she was interred, there was no ceremony conducted to pray for the deceased or to ask that her soul be granted eternal rest.[2]

It was this lack of respect, and the absence of last rites, so says the legend, which causes the young woman's wraith to rise from her grave on the anniversary of her death. Once out into the night air it is said she then sits on her tombstone and weeps. Her despondency was caused, perhaps, because she sees that strange epitaph on her headstone and is reminded of the unceremonious way she was buried.

On the other hand, maybe she is still envious of the respect shown to General Benner at his funeral. It was said to be the longest funeral procession ever seen in the area; so long, in fact, that "when the hearse reached the graveyard in the field, the last carriage of the procession had not left the mansion."[3]

Although the weeping ghost of Rock Cemetery, if indeed such an entity exists, is to be pitied for the lonely lament she has to repeat year after year, she is not unique in that respect.

One of the more popular accounts about graveyard ghosts, that is still told and retold in the Pennsylvania Dutch regions of southeastern

2. Myrtle Magargel, *The History of Rock*, 69, 78.
3. Thornton Wheeler, "Philip Benner and the Political Press," *Town and Gown Magazine*, February 1980.

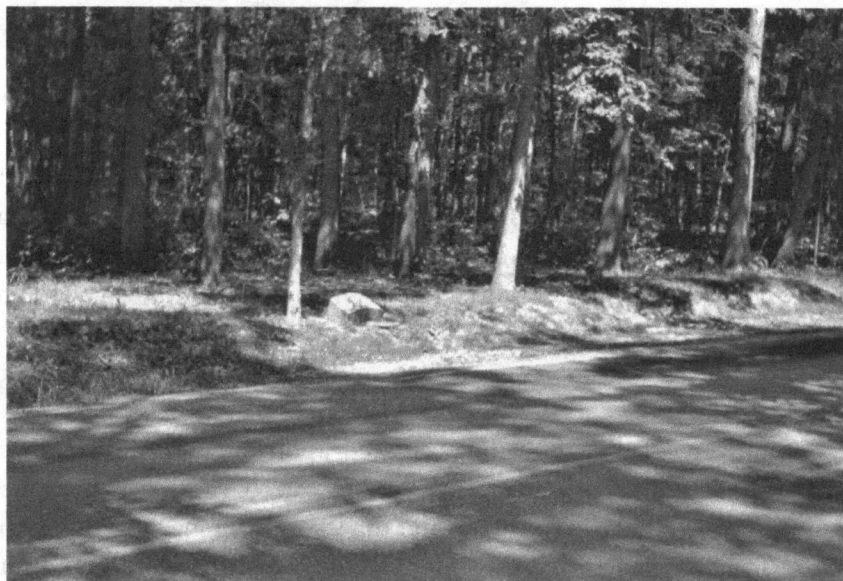

Clara Price's lonely memorial and the shady woods behind it . Along Route 879, between Pine Glen and Karthaus, Centre County.

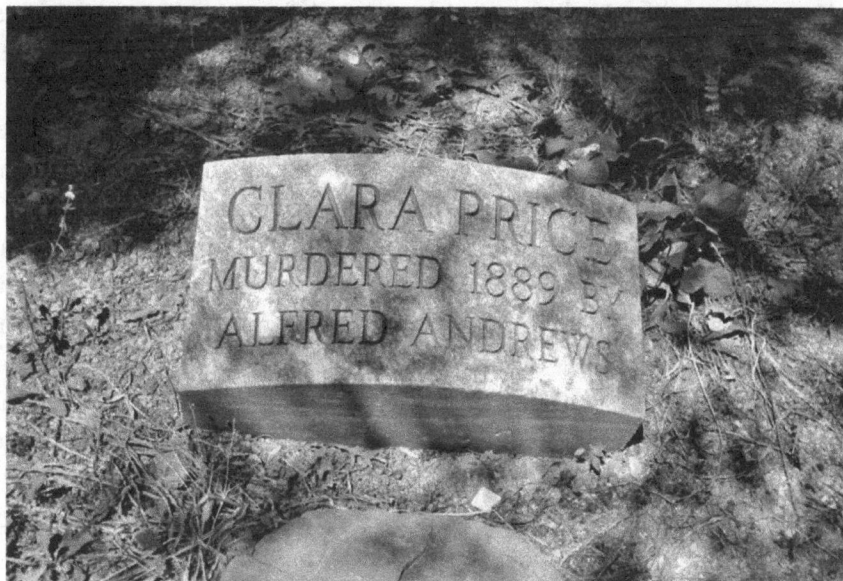

Inscription on the Clara Price Memorial.

Pennsylvania, deals with another young lady whose hopes and dreams were also stolen away from her at a young age and at a moment of great promise in her life. However, in this case, the young woman's "ghost" is said to appear in a very different way than the vaporous form usually ascribed to visitors from the land of the dead.

Even though she died almost a century ago, the story of Augusta Bitner's tragic death and her ghostly appearances still intrigue those who hear her sad tale. It is often repeated now and then in hushed tones by residents who live next to the old cemetery along Lemon Street in the city of Lancaster, Lancaster County. Here, within the city's hallowed ground, stands a monument to this Victorian-age woman, and both its size and its detail are enough to attract the curious.

Reminiscent of the stone effigies placed upon the graves of Medieval royals in England, the life-size statue in Lancaster Cemetery was created for the same purpose—so the living and the yet unborn may gaze upon the likeness and know what the person looked like when still alive, and, more importantly, to pray for the deceased's acceptance into the heavenly realm.

Then, too, Augusta's parents must have thought that their sorrows would be more readily assuaged if they could come to her burial spot and see an erect life-size likeness of her, even if it was just a stone image. Regardless of their reason, the grieving couple spared no expense when they erected the monument to their daughter's memory. If nothing else, it is apparent they could not easily cast aside their deep grief and sorrow over her untimely passing. This was because, you see, on that terrible day she died it was to be a special day. It was to be Augusta's wedding day.

Maybe she was modeling her wedding gown or just wearing a long dress typical of the Victorian Age, but whatever the case, it was perhaps the long garment that she was wearing that caused her to trip and fall down the stairs of her parents' house that fateful day in 1906.

Too much time has passed since then, to be able to find anyone who now remembers the exact details of her demise, and, in fact, another version of the legend says the young lady died of tuberculosis instead of a nasty fall, but all who repeat the story do agree that on the anniversary of her death, Augusta's spirit makes its presence known.

According to the legendary accounts that can be heard yet today, Augusta Bitner's restless soul is not content to appear in the form of a barely discernable mist. Apparently so distraught at being pulled out of the world at such a young and tender age, and so disconsolate at not being able to feel her betrothed hold her in his arms once again, Augusta has decided to materialize in a more "concrete" way.

It is for this reason, claim the tellers of the tale, that it is not a vaporous non-solid apparition that manifests itself on the anniversary of her death. Instead, she has chosen a way she can display her longing to return to earth in a solid human form once again.

Alfred Andrews. (Photo found on the Internet at www.bellefonte. topcities.com/hangings/page5.html.)

The reason that people may reach this conclusion about Augusta Bitner's tormented soul is because some believe her concrete statue becomes mobile and walks around the graveyard on the night of the anniversary of her death.

Apparently, the lifelike form knows not where to go and just wanders aimlessly, winding its way past the cemetery's many other monuments to departed souls, but as the first faint streaks of dawn begin to penetrate the night sky, the statue somehow finds its way back to its pedestal.

Then when the full light of day finally comes, the concrete likeness freezes back into place once again and no one is any wiser as to its alleged nocturnal perambulations. However, there were those who once believed they knew the statue's secret, and it was those folks who gave it the name that it goes by today—the Walking Ghost of Lancaster Cemetery.[4]

Up in northeastern Clearfield County, near the historic village of Karthaus, there once lived another woman who also met an untimely death, but her demise was not due to illness or accident. In this case her life was snuffed out by human hands, and, so claim local tales, her soul is also a restless one because of the terrible way in which it met its end when in human form.

Where the West Branch of the Susquehanna forms the boundary line of Clearfield and Centre Counties, there are a number of villages that sit tucked away and almost forgotten in remote valleys formed by ridges and spurs of the Allegheny Front. Among these small towns are places like Pine

---

4. Rick Fisher, recorded July 1997.

Glen, Frenchville, Keewaydin, and Pottersdale, and each little hamlet has its share of local legends and its tales of local characters.

However, all these parochial anecdotes were quickly forgotten, one November day back in 1889, when a sensational murder occurred in Burnside Township of Centre County, just across the Clearfield County Line near Karthaus.

No doubt the news of the tragic event traveled rapidly for those days, with folks in The Knobs country to the south and over Chestnut Ridge

Graveyard at Huff's Church, Berks County. (See the author's Volume 4 and the chapter titled "Mans' Best Friend [ly ghost]" for a haunting tale from this section of the Keystone State.)

to the west perhaps learning of the events in record time. It was, after all, a remarkable occurrence for that age, this murder of an innocent young woman by a local man who shot her and left her dying on the highway. And there was no proof, other than circumstantial evidence, to ensure that the guilty party could be convicted. Nevertheless, in the end justice prevailed and Clara Price's killer paid the ultimate price for his crime.

Alfred Andrews had been on the wrong side of the law since he came to the United States from England, and on this 27th day of November in 1889, he was heading for bigger trouble. He had come up to Karthaus from his hometown of Brisbin, Clearfield County, to settle some debts that day, and he had murder on his mind.

He owed money to three people in Karthaus, and in his warped way of thinking he had decided that the best way to get out of debt was to kill all three, including the person to whom he owed fifty cents. It was early enough that he had not planned on there being anyone on the road into Karthaus that morning, and when he came upon an attractive woman, he panicked. He wanted no witnesses to his comings or goings that day.

Clara Price had been hired by the Eugene Meeker family as a cleaning woman and family helper, and today she had decided to take a day off to visit her parents and do some shopping in Karthaus. It was an unfortunate choice, for later that same morning three other travelers found her lying face down on the highway, her body still warm and blood running from her mouth. Upon further inspection, however, it was determined she had been shot, and her life had already drained away.

Although hard evidence was missing, there were locals along the road who testified that they had seen Clara Price pass by their houses that morning, and shortly afterwards had seen Andrews pass by too, heading in the same direction. Based on this testimony and on other evidence, the authorities were able to wring a confession out of Andrews.

After six days of hearings that took place in Bellefonte during January 1890, the defendant was found guilty of murder in the first degree and sentenced accordingly.[5] Judge Austin O. Furst handed down the sentence to the prisoner in an address that was considered by his legal peers "as an expression of high order of thought and language."[6]

---

5. Roberta Firestone, recorded April 1, 2001.
6. J. H. Beers and Co., *Commemorative Biographical Record of Central Pennsylvania*, 53.

Furst showed no mercy, sentencing Andrews to death by hanging in the Bellefonte jail yard and ending his penalty announcement with the age-old plea of "and may God have mercy upon your soul."[7] After the execution on May 9, 1890, Andrews' body was taken to a hillside cemetery in Bellefonte and buried in an unmarked grave.

Today no one probably knows the location of Andrews' final resting place, but he apparently reposes there peacefully since there have never been any reports that his ghost haunts the hillside where he was buried. Clara Price, on the other hand, has not been so lucky, at least if legendary accounts are accepted as fact.

Although she lies in a small cemetery in Keewaydin and has an appropriate stone to mark her grave, there are those who say that Clara Price's spirit is a restless one due to the violent way in which her life on earth ended. However, it is not the cemetery in Keewaydin, Clearfield County, where Clara's shade supposedly appears. Instead, the spot where her apparition materializes, some believe, is the spot where she was gunned down by the merciless Andrews.

Along Route 879, between Pine Glen and Karthaus, there is a stone monument that will escape the attention of passing motorists unless they look closely for it. Since it is only about six inches high, the small tablet sitting alongside the road on the road bank is easy to miss. Nonetheless, it is this memorial that commemorates the site of Clara Price's murder in the woods behind the marker.

There are many misconceptions about the marker, which is inscribed with the words "Clara Price, Murdered 1889 by Alfred Andrews." Many think that it marks the site of the unfortunate woman's grave, but she is buried in Keewaydin. Others think the shooting occurred here on this same road, but back then the road passed through the woods behind the stone that holds the inscription recalling Clara's death.

And it is in those woods that the last essences of Clara Price's spirit sometimes coalesce into the ghostly form that some say can be seen floating through the dark forest during a cold winter dawn of late November. One such near-witness, according to a popular local tale, was a motorist who was forced to make an unplanned stop here one night.

The young driver's tire went flat, which usually wouldn't be a problem for him. However, when the excitable motorist realized where he was, he

---

7. Ibid.

Fairview Church and cemetery, Curtin Hollow, Centre County. It is on the side of this church, claim locals, that on nights of a full moon, an image of a pig hanger appears to serve as a reminder of its use as a scaffold for a murderer who was tried and hanged here by frontier vigilantes sometime in the nineteenth century.

began to have second thoughts. It was late at night, very dark, and the spot was uncomfortably lonely. There was little or no traffic passing by at this late hour, and then the stranded driver began to recall the stories of Clara's ghost and how it would sometimes appear here.

It was an interesting and intriguing tale, and it had seemed to many that it might be fun to see the ghost, but now that he was in a situation where he might actually come face to face with the specter, the man decided the flat tire could wait until morning. Starting off at a rapid clip, he walked the rest of the way into Karthaus that night, never once looking back.[8]

Although Alfred Andrews' spirit apparently has made its peace with the Creator, there are others who claim there is another restless phantom that haunts a small country church in Centre County because it has not found a way to atone for similar sins. Like Andrews, this man's life (his name, if he ever existed, is no longer remembered) also ended by hanging, punishment for a murder he committed in the valley where he lived during a period that can only now be pinpointed as sometime "in the 1800s."

His hanging was apparently not an official one since it is described more like a form of vigilante or frontier justice than a legally sanctioned

8. Ann Eminhizer, letter dated November 6, 1997.

execution. Nonetheless, things like that apparently did sometimes happen in earlier days if folktales and legends can be believed (see the author's story called "Rafting Days" in *Volume I*).

According to the legend that centers around the Fairview Church in Curtin Hollow north of Milesburg, the local citizenry took it upon themselves to track down and imprison a man who had committed a foul murder in that section.

The area was still isolated enough during those days that the "long arm of the law" didn't extend that far too often, if at all, and so the consensus was that rather than wait for the legal system to take action, the valley folk should take matters into their own hands.

So, one summer day a group of men erected a tall tripod consisting of three sturdy timber poles near the local churchyard where the current Fairview Church building now stands. Next, they securely fastened a rope at the top of the tripod and then tied a noose at the other end. Normally such a construction would be called a "pig hanger" since it was usually used for hanging up pigs during butchering season, but now it was used for a darker purpose.

Placing the noose around the "convicted" man's neck, they hanged him on the spot. A full moon rose in the sky that night, casting an eerie light on the burial party as they lowered the dead man's body into an unmarked grave, somewhere in the loneliest and deepest hollow of the nearby hills.

Now, so claim some locals, on the night of the anniversary of the hanging if the moon is full, the shadow of the pig hanger appears on the side of the church. Perhaps it is in this way that the troubled spirit seeks forgiveness or some prayers for an end to its unquiet existence. Until it gets such help, it apparently will remain just another one of Pennsylvania's many ghosts of the graveyard.[9]

NOTE: In order to take the story of Augusta Bitner one step past what other writers have done with it, I attempted to obtain a copy of her death certificate to see what cause of death might be listed on it. The year 1906 is the earliest year that the state of Pennsylvania has records of its residents' deaths. Since Augusta died in 1906, it seemed as though her death certificate should be on file. However, the response to my request for that

9. Don Rocky, interviewed July 31, 2000.

certificate was as follows: "This is to certify that based on the information provided, the Division of Vital Records has been unable to locate a record of this death."[10]

Unfortunately, it therefore appears that we will never know how Augusta really died. Someday perhaps she herself will reveal that secret to someone; a person who has sufficient courage to linger there long enough on a night that Augusta's spirit or her statue decides to promenade through the Lancaster Cemetery along Lemon Street.

---

10. Department of Vital Records, New Castle, PA, letter dated December 29, 2005.

CHAPTER 3

WAR WHOOP AND SCALPING KNIFE

Pennsylvania's many years of border warfare, when the indigenous population was trying to prevent European colonists from stealing ancestral land that the Native Americans considered to be theirs and theirs alone, has been described as a thrilling and romantic chapter in the state's history. On the other hand, that period of time would hardly have been described as romantic by the settlers who endured the sufferings and woes that accompanied those terrible decades.

The terrifying sound of the warrior's war whoop, scalped relatives, kidnapped wives and children, and burning homesteads and barns were things that affected the lives and shattered the dreams of the hardiest frontiersmen of that age; events very similar to the traumas experienced by hurricane and earthquake victims of this modern era. However, there are more than just historical parallels that remind us of a time in Pennsylvania's history that, for those who experienced it firsthand, might more aptly be called chilling and melancholic instead of thrilling and romantic.

Those decades of heartbreak and desolation that comprise Pennsylvania's epoch of border warfare appear to have occurred so far back in the distant past that it seems impossible to reconnect with them in a way that is meaningful for us today. Ideally, we could somehow place ourselves in that space and time so we could observe events at a safe distance and actually feel what it was like to have lived through them; to experience it for ourselves.

The Sierer Farm, as seen from Route 192 near Buffalo Crossroads, Union County.

That's, of course, not possible, and so we must be content with reading about those days in history books and novels of historical fiction, or by viewing movies and reenactments based upon them. On the other hand, there are ways to connect with that period in an even closer way, and this chapter will lead the reader to a few of those links; avenues that prove that the past is really never that far away after all.

In the writer's second volume of this series (*The Black Ghost of Scotia, and More Pennsylvania Fireside Tales*), there is a chapter titled "The Lower Fort," and in that chapter there is an account of the massacre of the Jacob Standford family near the "Upper" or Potters Fort in Potter Township of Centre County on the morning of May 8, 1778. Some details concerning that terrible event were preserved for posterity through a deposition made by express rider Robert Moore, who discovered the bodies of Jacob Standford, his wife, and their daughter, lying by the spring that still bubbles up yet today from the hallowed ground upon which the Standfords were slain. However, no such depositions were ever obtained from members of the Standford family themselves because, of course, they were all massacred, except for their son Abraham, who was taken captive.

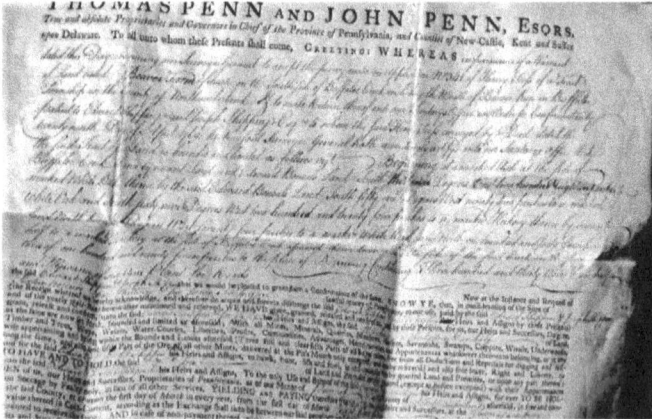

Original deed to the Sierer farm. Deeded from the sons of William Penn to Joseph and Edward Shippen in 1705.

It is bad enough that the bodies of his parents and sister lie in lost and forgotten gravesites in a corner of a field near their cabin (still standing today in the same spot where Jacob Standford built it), but historians also lament the fact that no one could get a deposition from the sole survivor of the massacre.

After being carried off by a war party, it might be said that ten-year-old Abraham's fate was lost in the swirling woodsmoke and glittering sparks of an aborigine campfire, and as a result there are no words or recollections from the lips of any member of the Standford family that came down to us through the historical record. Nonetheless, fate has a way of setting that record straight at times, and so it has with the life of Abraham Standford.

Five years after I had published the second volume in my series, I was put in touch with a man in Texas who traced his lineage back to the long-lost Abraham Standford. The gentleman had been fortunate as a child to be able to sit at the knee of his great-grandmother as she "enchanted" him with many anecdotes about Pennsylvania frontier life during the Revolutionary War, tales she had heard older members of her family tell when she, as a young child, sat at their knees and was enchanted by the tales as well. And those older folks should have known the facts; they heard the tales from Robert Standford, Abraham Standford's son.

According to the family lore, Abraham eventually escaped from his captors, members of the Iroquois Confederation, most likely Shawnee or

Clockface on the Sierer Homestead. Buffalo Township, Union County.

Delaware, and settled first in present-day Westmoreland County. Later the former captive moved to Clarion County Pennsylvania where he raised his family.

And it was here that he passed on to his children the tales of the Pennsylvania frontier he had experienced firsthand. Among those delightful reminiscences were stories about the days prior to his capture; pleasant memories of the time he spent with his family during the first ten years of his life at the Standford cabin.

The warriors that came to the Standford homestead on that balmy day in May in 1778 would not have initially caused concern to the Standfords had they seen them, at least if Abraham Standford's memory served him well. According to him, Indian visitors to the cabin were commonplace and the visits friendly ones. Sometimes, he recalled, those visitors even brought fresh venison along with them so the Standfords would have meat for their growing family.

The burly natives' motives, however, may not have been entirely altruistic. The dusky warriors, Abraham would later tell his own children, were very fond of Mrs. Standford's porridge and often asked her to make it. Given their fondness for the hot cereal, they may even have expected it as barter in return for their venison.

Regardless of how friendly those local Native Americans may have been, Abraham recalled the fear they instilled in him and his sister, when Jacob and his wife would invite these dark and mysterious sons of the forest to spend the night. And sometimes the kindly Standfords would tell their aboriginal neighbors that rather than hike back to their rude huts in the mountains in harsh weather, they were welcome to curl up on the floor with their heads toward the warm fireplace and sleep there.

The children had their beds in the loft of the cabin, a place that must have usually felt like a cozy and safe haven above the troubles of the world below. However, when the Indians slept on the floor right under their very heads, Abraham and his sister "were scared all night."[1]

The Standfords should have perhaps been more attuned to their children's fears, as should have the other settlers around them. At least Colonel James Potter seemed to realize that more trouble was on the way after the Standfords were killed. Writing from the Upper Fort in Penn's Valley on the 17th of May 1778, he sent a note to colonial authorities indicating that "Our savage enemy continues to murder, scalp, and capture. If there is not something done, the country will be entirely given up to them."[2]

Then, in July of that same year, settlers harvesting grain in fields east of Potters Fort were attacked by a party of five warriors, and two soldiers guarding the reapers were killed in the encounter (see the chapter titled "Burned at the Stake" in the author's second volume for the unusual tale linked to this episode). Numerous raids all along the Pennsylvania frontier during those hot sultry days of the Independence Month finally precipitated

1. Robert Weilacher, telephone conversation, September 21, 2002.
2. Linn, Ibid, 20.

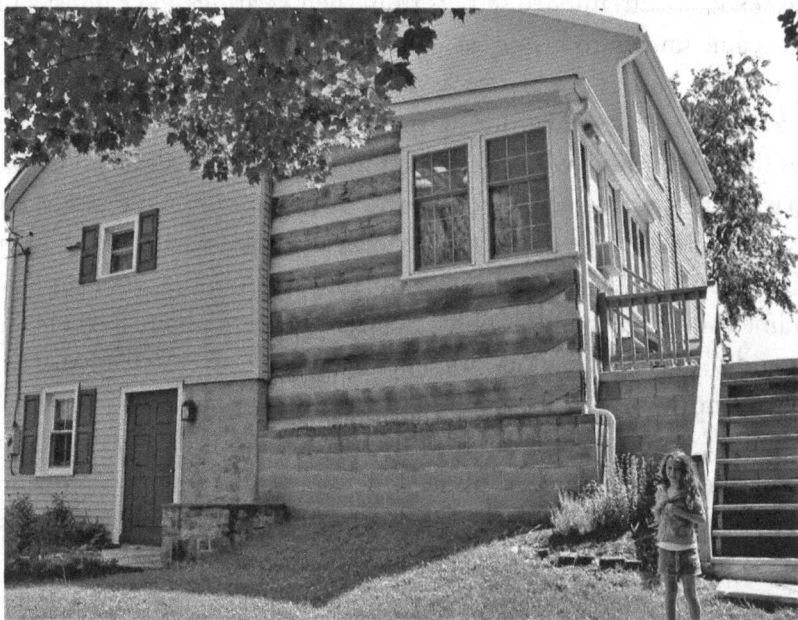

The Sierers' Original Log Cabin. Still standing and used as a family home today.

The Flax Field. Still an open field behind the Sierer Cabin, this was the field where the Sierers hid from Indian marauders.

a mass exodus of frightened settlers from their clearings and cabins; a flight that became known to history as "The Great Runaway."

Fearsome parties of warriors were not always successful in their surprise attacks upon frontiersmen during the time of the Great Runaway. Sometimes there were those who risked their lives to raise the alarm about bands of marauding warriors about to swoop down upon the settlements; and it was early warnings like this that gave settlers ample time to flee to safety.

The most notable example of a similar alarm-sounder was Paul Revere, his fame assured through Longfellow's classic poem about Revere's "midnight ride." But Revere's ride was to warn of the approach of the King's Redcoats, not war parties. Then too, Revere was a man.

Hanging on the wall inside the Post Office in Muncy, Lycoming County, there is a tribute to another rider who carried news of impending danger. However this tribute is in the form of a mural, and it was placed there not to honor a man, but rather to honor a woman. Hanging beside that oil painting, commissioned by the Post Office Department and drawn

Colonel John Kelly's homestead the way it looks today. Buffalo Township, Union County.

there by John Beauchamp in 1938, is a plaque that explains what the colorful portrayal is all about.

Those who take the time to read the plaque will realize just how unique the multi-colored painting is since it is one of the few art works commissioned by the Post Office that depicts a woman doing anything heroic.

"Rachel Silverthorn's Ride," the title given to the post office oil painting, depicts a young woman on a beautiful white horse as she warns the settlers along Muncy Creek, Lycoming County, that they are in danger of being attacked by marauding warriors that had ambushed and killed a number of settlers and soldiers at the mouth of Loyalsock Creek that very morning. Included among those victims was young James Brady, son of Captain John Brady, the man George Washington had sent to the Susquehanna Valley to organize a group of volunteers for protection of the area.

Washington could spare no troops for that task, and so was counting on Captain Brady to organize a defense. As part of those efforts, Brady had started construction of a frontier fort that he named Fort Muncy and that work was still underway when in the early afternoon of August 8, 1778, a lone survivor of the Loyalsock Creek massacre straggled into the bastion.

Realizing that those same raiding parties would attack settlements along Muncy Creek next, Brady asked for a volunteer to ride up the stream and warn settlers of their danger. Not a man stepped forward, even after the captain offered his own white mare for the perilous ride. Then from out of the back of the group stepped a young woman.

The Bradys' many bold and heroic deeds in fighting fierce warriors in the West Branch Valley are not only legendary but are also well-documented in the historical annals of that tradition-steeped region. The same cannot, however, be said for the heroic ride made by Rachel Silverthorn on the eighth day of August in 1778. All the men present at Fort Muncy that afternoon must have been momentarily stunned; too surprised to stop her when the pretty young woman stepped forward and then leapt upon the back of John Brady's steed and rode off.

History does not record what her rewards might have been after she returned safely from her ride, but probably just the heartfelt thanks of the many settlers, who later slipped safely into the fort under cover of darkness that night, was reward enough for this unsung heroine. And it is because her memory is not preserved in the history books that I decided to

Kelly's Spring, where Colonel Kelly shot the Indian hiding behind a tree.

include her story here.[3] Additionally the tale also affords an opportunity to mention the unfortunate fact that there was not a heroine like Rachel in neighboring Union County two years later.

Living due north of Penn's Creek in present-day Limestone Township of Union County in 1780 was a family named Watson. The Watsons had built their cabin on a little elevation near the place called White Springs, an ideal spot where crystal clear waters poured forth from cool mountain depths.

---

3. Details on Rachel Silverthorn's ride taken from a plaque that hangs under the painting of the same name and which is mounted on the wall of the Post Office in Muncy, PA. August, 2005.

Colonel Kelly's gravestone in the Lewisburg Cemetery, Union County. A prominent monument to this noteworthy patriot and original settler.

It must have always seemed like an idyllic location to the family, but late one warm summer day in July the tranquility of the nearby woods was broken by the sound of advancing moccasined marauders as their feet crushed the dried leaves of the forest floor. Then as dusk cast a deathly pallor over the gaps and glens of Penn's Creek Mountain to the south, the sounds of gunfire pierced the afternoon stillness.

Apparently only eighty-year-old Elizabeth Watson and her son Patrick were at the homestead on that particular afternoon, because neither written historical accounts nor the family's oral history mention any other family members when recalling the incident. However, the memories of that sad event that have been preserved as they were told and retold down through many generations of the Watsons' descendants do add some details about Mrs. Watson's death that are not mentioned in the historical record.

According to that historical record, Christian Shively, the Watson's nearest neighbor, heard the shots that July afternoon in 1780, and carrying his flintlock rifle, immediately rushed to the Watson clearing to determine if the family was safe. The old settler was greeted by a sickening sight, also described in the written account. Lying on the cabin floor was Mrs. Watson. She had been shot and scalped, and the family dog was licking the blood from her head.

She lived only long enough to indicate that her son Patrick had gone "down the run." When Shively found Patrick along the cool waters, the dying man told him he hadn't realized he had been shot until he stooped down, took a drink, and saw the water run out of the bullet hole in his wound. He, too, expired soon afterwards.[4]

Although the historical description of the Watson massacre paints a picture of how fearless and tough the settlers of those times had to be, it does not go far enough, if the oral historical accounts about the same event are to be believed. Watsons' descendants, for example, say that Mrs. Watson was at the White Spring getting water when she was stunned by the musket ball that hit her.

Falling to the ground she could only lay there helplessly as her assailants walked up to her, calmly cut off her scalp, and left her for dead. However, the hardy woman, according to the oral history, still managed to drag herself from the spring back into her cabin, which, in her dying state, must have seemed to be a place of relative safety. And it was there that Christian Shively found her.

The Watson cabin, greatly remodeled and now covered with siding, still stands today on its original site. As such, it not only still serves as home to a kindly family of Old Order Mennonites; but also as one of those surviving links to a yesteryear that is both amazing and, at the same time, appalling. Likewise, not only has the oral history of the Watson family, if true, preserved an account of how valiantly Mrs. Watson tried to save

---

4. John Blair Linn, *Annals of Buffalo Valley Pennsylvania*, 188–89; C. Hale Sipe, *Indian Wars of Pennsylvania*, 619.

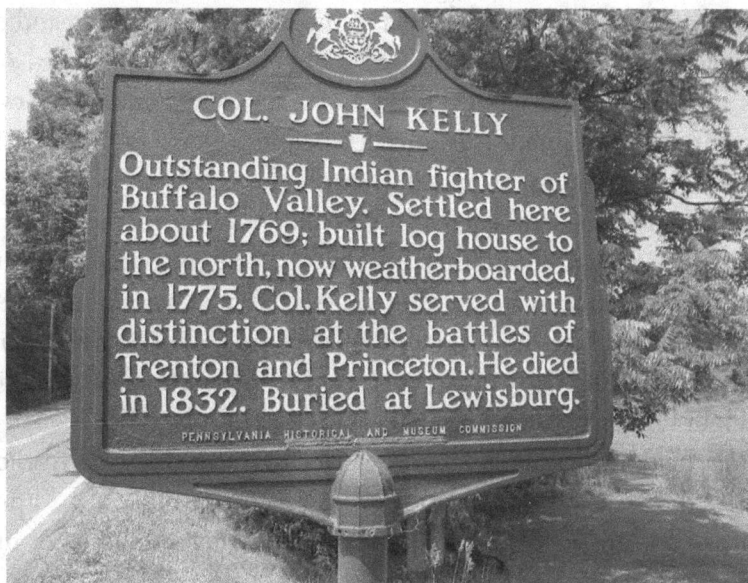

Historical marker at Colonel John Kelly's Homestead.

herself after being shot and scalped that day, but it also has brought her first name down to us through a span of over two hundred years.[5]

That forename was not preserved in any written accounts of her death at the hands of the attacking warriors, but now that her full name is recorded in this book, Mrs. Elizabeth Watson has a good chance of escaping the fate of many other victims of Pennsylvania's border wars whose names will never be known. On the other hand, there are some victims of those wars who are guaranteed to be remembered, not only because their names have been preserved in the historical record, but also because those same names have been engraved into stone monuments that commemorate their tragic fate.

Down in the South Mountains of Franklin County, in present-day Antrim Township and just three miles northwest of the attractive and invit- ing town of Greencastle, there was once a little country schoolhouse that served as the seat of learning for about a dozen scholars back in colonial times.

Schoolmaster Enoch Brown was the teacher of this small group of settlers' children, and although their schoolhouse no longer exists today, there is a large and little-visited monument that does mark the place where the building once stood. Engraved upon the tall stone is a dedication that

---

5. David Reed, interviewed January 8, 2006.

explains that the memorial is "Sacred to the memory" of Brown and eleven of his students. The names of five of those students were placed on the obelisk as well, but the names of the other six were "unknown," even in 1885 when the monument was unveiled before a crowd of 5,000 people.

At first the monument and its sentiments might seem delightful, a colorful reminder of times past, but further reading of the inscriptions upon it will lead one to another conclusion. The memorial, surrounded by a sturdy iron fence, was not, after all, erected merely to mark the site of a colonial schoolhouse. It is in fact a tombstone identifying the common grave of schoolmaster Brown and the eleven scholars who died with him on what might have otherwise been a pleasant day in July 1764.

It was then, during the time now referred to by historians as The Pontiac War, after the great Ottawa chieftain who organized and led the uprising, that Brown and his scholars met a fate that stretched the limits of human debauchery even for those bloody times.

Described by the great colonial historian Francis Parkman as "an outrage unmatched in fiend-like atrocity through all the annals of the war,"[6] the murder and scalping of Brown and all his students by warring marauders that summer day left the entire valley in mourning, for it was said that each student came from a different family.

The young warriors who committed the atrocity made a hasty retreat by following Conococheague Creek into Path Valley and then over the mountains to their villages. They expected to be regaled for their bloody deeds, especially since they brought back scalps of their victims, but once their chiefs learned what they had done, they ridiculed them.

Taken aback by the cowardly act, the chiefs refused to praise the treacherous young warriors, especially after they learned that Brown had tried to bargain with them, offering his life and scalp in return for the lives of the little ones; nine boys and two girls, in his charge.

Not one of those children's lives had been spared, or so thought the killers, but there was a survivor, and another marker was erected on this hallowed ground to preserve his memory as well.

Standing along a dark and gloomy cut in the mountain, just south of the schoolhouse site, is a small bronze plaque that marks the site of "Archie

---

6. Warner, Beers and Co., *History of Franklin County, Pennsylvania*, 172; and Francis Parkman, *Conspiracy of Pontiac*, 278.

McCullough's Spring," and it is by this plaque that one can see the water that bubbles up here and turns into a fast-flowing creek. The stream makes a pleasant sound as it cascades over the moss-covered rocks and small pebbles that line the bottom of the ravine, and it certainly must have been an inviting place to play for Enoch Brown's students in those times.

Perhaps the ravine's cool zephyrs and soothing mists were a welcome relief during hot summer days, or maybe its dark shadows provided just the right amount of romance and mystery that students were drawn to it, but whatever the case, Archie McCullough seemed to think he could find solace there on the day the murdering wretches fell upon him, his fellow students, and schoolmaster Enoch Brown. For it was here, according to the plaque, that horrified settlers found Archie "trying to wash the clotted blood from his face and scalpless head."[7]

The little boy survived the attack, but he never fully recovered; his emotional wounds being too deep. History does not record how many years the unfortunate child lived after he was found at the spring that infamous day, but his mind was never the same, and he was left in a condition described by historians as "somewhat demented."[8]

Franklin County's monument and memorial plaque to Enoch Brown and his students do provide another, more personal, link to those perilous times in Pennsylvania's history when the indigenous population and colonial settlers were at war, thereby enabling us to experience them in a closer way. However, those reminders are gruesome ones, and for those who would like something more positive, there is a remarkable memorial over in Union County that might be more to their liking, and which also provides another tangible link back to the time of the war whoop and scalping knife.

Sitting off the beaten path, at the end of a long country lane beside Beaver Run in Buffalo Township of Union County, near the quaintly-named village of Buffalo Crossroads, there is an ancient stone farmhouse, built over 200 years ago, that evokes a nostalgic feeling in those who pass by the old place.

Perhaps it is the size of the trees that stand in the front yard that provide a clue as to the age of the homestead, or maybe it's just the old-time

7. Warner, Beers and Co., *History of Franklin County, Pennsylvania*, 172–174; and details copied by the author from the plaque at Archie McCullough's Spring, during a visit there in October 2005.
8. C. Hale Sipe, *The Indian Wars of Pennsylvania*, 473.

View of the Patrick Watson farmhouse and spring; still a working farm as of 2006. Limestone Township, Union County

architecture that conveys the same message, but whatever the case, it is a delight to behold. Even more so when a closer look is taken at the east face of the house and the eyes wander up to the roof top.

Here, located just under the roof peak, are two stones that are different than the other field stones that were used to build the manor house, for on both these stones there are inscriptions and engravings that turned the monoliths into memorials of another, more deadly, time.

The lowest block is rectangular in shape and is engraved with the letters "J H S 1795 S N S," which, according to the present owner of the picturesque farm, records the year the house was built and the initials of the husband and wife who built it, Johannes and Susannah Sierer. Then just above the rectangular stone is a square one with a more ambiguous engraving upon it; an engraving assured to mystify and intrigue anyone who sees it.

The date on the square block, 1795, also commemorates the date the place was built, but below that date is a clock face, complete with Roman numerals, and an hour and a minute hand set to exactly 11:45. Fortunately the reason the odd decoration was added to the square date stone has been faithfully preserved by the farm's string of owners over the years.

When the new owner of the farm takes over, he is also given two other things. First is the original deed to the farm that was conveyed to Edward and Joseph Shippen by Thomas and John Penn, sons of William Penn, in 1705. The legal language inked upon the thick parchment in flowery black lettering is amazing to behold and only adds to the value of this remarkable artifact, which is always cherished by the farm's owners.

In addition to that original deed, the second thing that buyers are given when they purchase the farm, the story of the clock face, is something the new owners appreciate almost as much as that remarkable deed, since both date back to colonial times.

The story of the clock face was told to us one cold winter day when the friendly farmer who currently owns the place took time from his barn chores to pause a minute and take our minds back once again to the time of the Great Runaway. In addition to showing us the aforementioned deed, the young man also recalled the event that led to the engraving of the clock face on that square stone in the east face of the Sierer's mansion.

According to our storyteller, the Sierers didn't originally live here. At the time of the Great Runaway in 1778, the family residence was an old log cabin just a short distance south of the present house. Part of that old cabin can still be seen today, across from the farm on the other side of Route 192, but modern additions and siding have hidden most of the original logs.

It was here, one night in 1778, that the Sierer's dog, a gift given to the Sierer's daughters by a kind neighbor that day, began barking and fussing enough that the Sierers became alarmed. Looking outside they could with the aid of sufficient moonlight discern, across one of their fields and as yet at some distance, a band of savage warriors trying to sneak up on the unsuspecting family. The dog's timely warning gave the settlers just enough time to make a stealthy exit out the back of the cabin and hide in a flax field on a hill behind the house.

Upon finding the homestead empty, the war party vented their frustrations by ransacking the place, which apparently tired them out so much that they left without making sufficient effort to determine whether any of the cabin's former inhabitants were still in the area or not.

Mural of Rachel Silverthorn's Ride. (United States Post Office, Muncy, Lycoming County)

The Sierers must have felt it was God himself who had intervened on their behalf that night, and that was something that they didn't want to forget. In order to ensure that they did not, they decided to engrave a clock face on the date stone of their new house. The time they decided to put on that face was 11:45—the precise moment their dog had warned them of the warring marauders that were coming to kill them and carry away their scalps.[9]

As it turned out, the Sierers did not have the only dog in Buffalo Valley that saved its owners from certain destruction at the hands of a warrior death squad. During that same period one of the valley's other settlers was lucky enough to have a canine sentinel that performed a similar good deed.

Living in Buffalo Valley at the same time as the Sierers was Colonel John Kelly, a close neighbor and a hero of the Revolutionary War. Famous for thwarting a British advance by leading the detail that destroyed the bridge over Stony Brook near Worth's Mills New Jersey in 1777, Colonel Kelly was also acclaimed, at least according to local folktales, as the slayer of the last woods bison in the state of Pennsylvania.

It is from these extinct animals that some think the name of the valley was derived as well as that of the village of Buffalo Crossroads. Likewise, Kelly Township, and the small town of Kelly Crossroads in the same

9. David Reed and Curtis Brubaker, interviewed January 8, 2006.

county, were named in honor of the Colonel, who was also noted as one of the valley's staunchest defenders during the time of the Great Runaway.

Most of the inhabitants of Buffalo Valley, fearing further war party incursions, abandoned their homes in the summer of 1779. Only the bravest landholders, including Colonel Kelly, stayed behind to protect their cabins, and faithfully standing guard with his master was Kelly's dog.

It was this dog that awakened Kelly early one morning with its growling, a warning which enabled Kelly to spot a lone Indian hiding in some bushes near his cabin. With a well-directed musket ball, which "passed clear through the warrior's head," Kelly managed to kill his adversary before the hidden sniper was able to execute his surprise attack.[10]

History doesn't record whether the Colonel erected any special memorial to his canine savior when it died, but it's certainly plausible to think that Kelly never forgot the debt he owed to his little friend. He must have enjoyed telling of the episode when talking with friends like the Sierers, and valley traditions indicate that the first Thanksgiving celebration in Buffalo Valley was hosted by the Sierers, as were subsequent ones.

The Sierers always invited their nearest neighbors, including Colonel Kelly, to those feasts, and also made a point to extend invitations to the friendly Native Americans that remained in the area. No doubt the presence of the peaceful Indians brought back memories of the Great Runaway to the Colonel and to Johannes Sierer, and among the things the two men would have enjoyed talking about were how both of them owed their lives to their ever-vigilant watch dogs. Today, the clock face on the old stone house in Buffalo Valley serves as a reminder of one of those dogs as well as of the brave pioneers who settled the region.

INTERESTING HISTORICAL CORROBORATION

For those who are skeptical about the account of the Sierer family and their dog hiding from Indian marauders in a nearby flax field without being discovered because the dog remained uncharacteristically quiet, the following account from Westmoreland County may prove convincing:

"The summer of 1782 was the gloomiest in our pioneer history," writes historian John N. Boucher in his *History of Westmoreland County*. He also notes that the infamous Indian attack on Hannastown occurred July 13,

---

10. Linn, *Annals*, 172.

1782, the day after an ambush occurred on a nearby wedding party, he describes as follows:

"As the Indian troubles accumulated the pioneers became more and more united, until the summer of 1782 they nearly all lived in forts or blockhouses or in close proximity."

Despite the constant threat of marauding war parties, the pioneers were determined to carry on with their lives as normally as possible, including cementing the bonds of true love. As Boucher notes, "Love, like wild violets" continued to "blossom in the wilderness," and so on July 12, 1782, a wedding ceremony took place at Miller's Block-house near Hannastown, Westmoreland County. The event drew many people to it, such ceremonies being few and far between at that period. There were many young people and women there, and "there had been dancing to the tune of a fiddle, and playing and great glee among the guests, as was the custom in that day."

"Everything went off merrily until about the middle of the afternoon, when suddenly, like a peal of thunder from a cloudless sky, the war whoop burst upon their ears, and a band of savages rushed into their midst.

"Among those who escaped by flight was the daughter of Judge Hanna. She was taken on horseback by Samuel Findley, a pack-horse driver, and carried to the country, and thus escaped.

"A young man who had hastened to Miller's to give the alarm, in making his escape took with him a child. He was very soon pursued by three or four Indians who were gaining on him, although he could easily have distanced them in a foot race had he not been burdened by the child. This race was kept up for some time, and the young man's strength was rapidly waning.

"Fortunately, he came to a thick growth of underbrush, and beyond it was a high rail fence which bordered a field of uncut rye. He passed through the brush, mounted the fence, and jumped from the top of it as far into the rye field as he could. While in the brush and crossing the fence he was out of sight of the Indians. Then he lay down on the ground with the child, which fortunately kept quiet. The Indians came up and passed him without discovering him. They soon returned and looked more closely, but did not find him. Their time was necessarily brief, and they left with many mutterings of disgust."[11]

---

11. J. N. Boucher, *History of Westmoreland County, PA*, 171–79.

CHAPTER 4

HEXENHAMMER

Published in 1486, the treatise has been called "one of the most infamous books ever written," and "one of the most blood-soaked works in human history."[1] Although those statements may seem highly exaggerated, they are better understood when it's realized that the tome in question was a guidebook used by Inquisitors during the Inquisition.

Throughout that terrible period, which lasted from the fifteenth through the seventeenth centuries and encompassed many different parts of Europe, people could be brought to trial as an enemy of Christianity. Even worse, based upon the slimmest of reasons, and even less evidence, they could be sentenced to death in the Inquisitors' Court.

Reasons for a death sentence included heresy, alchemy, sorcery, and witchcraft, and those sentenced to die could expect to be burned alive at the stake or suffer an even worse demise. Estimates of the death toll during the 250 years of the Inquisition range from half a million to nine million, and many of those victims did die as accused witches.[2]

One such estimate states that "30,000 people suffered death as witches in England alone" during the era of the witchcraft hysteria.[3] Justifying that slaughter and the basis for it was a single book; a book that set forth the rules for identifying, prosecuting, and doing away with witches in the courts of the Inquisition. That book was the *Malleus Maleficarum*.

Said to have been written by two Dominican Inquisitors, the book became the witch hunter's "Bible," reaching such a level of popularity that

---

1. Wicasta Lovelace, "The Malleus Maleficarum of Heinrich Kramer and James Sprenger," found on the internet at www.malleus.maleficarum.org.
2. Ibid.
3. Charles Hardwick, *Traditions, Superstitions, and Folk-lore*, 100.

Typical Halloween image of a witch on her birch broomstick gliding across the face of a pale yellow moon on a cold dark All Souls Night. (Source: Freepik. Image by kjpargeter.)

it was at one time "second only to the Bible" in the total number of volumes sold.[4] Given the fact that the book was used as the official reference in the war on witchcraft, it's not surprising that its Latin title when translated into English means "The hammer of witches."

When translated into German, the title became *Hexenhammer*, and it was the ideas and descriptions in this volume that shaped and cemented European superstitions and fears about witches and witchcraft that immigrants to Pennsylvania brought with them from Germany in the 1730s.

Here in Pennsylvania, however, there was another book that could be called the Hexenhammer of the Pennsylvania Dutchmen. It was published in Reading in 1820 and became a reference that was just as popular as its European prototype, for someone deciding how to best protect themselves from witchcraft or to cast off an evil spell that had been placed upon them. The Reading edition was the first English version of the work and was titled *Pow-Wows or The Long Lost Friend.*

Written by self-styled healer John George Hohman, it was subtitled *A Collection of Mysterious Arts and Remedies for Man as well as Animals.* Many of the incantations and strange procedures outlined in the little manual were attributed to ancient sources, some even going as far back to Albertus

---

4. Lovelace, Ibid.

Magnus, German alchemist, magician, and Bishop of Regensburg in the thirteenth century.

Since the precepts in Hohman's book had origins that most likely dated back anywhere from two hundred to six hundred years, it is no wonder that they became so firmly entrenched in popular culture over the centuries. Consequently, they were so widely believed that even as late as the nineteenth century few people tended to question them. Gradually science and education eradicated those misconceptions, but even then, it took almost another 200 years to do so.

Much to my surprise, for example, back in 1970 when I began collecting the state's legends and folktales, I could still find, in the more remote sections of Pennsylvania, individuals who still believed in the old-time witches. One of the most memorable being the distinguished white-haired octogenarian who said to me in all seriousness (see the story titled "Hush Little Baby" in the author's first volume), "They say there's no such things as witches, but they'll never convince me of that!"[5]

Even along with those diehard believers who could still be found in the last decades of the twentieth century, there were many old-time witch tales that could still be collected as well. Moreover, in most cases these same stories usually contained thoughts and beliefs that seemed to be taken right from the pages of the *Hexenhammer* itself or from Hohman's Pennsylvania version, *The Long Lost Friend*. And one of the most notable things about the anecdotes was how often they repeated the same themes, or "motifs" as the folklorist likes to call them.

Typical of those motifs were many that were concerned with how best to protect oneself from a witch's evil spells, but they also often touched upon how a person could cast off those spells, if they couldn't prevent them in the first place. The old tales are still a source of fascination for us today, since they take us back to a remarkably different time and place. Among the most entertaining episodes of all of them are those containing vivid accounts of what measures people sometimes took to counteract a witch's evil intentions.

There were many things that people back then thought they could do to ward off evil spells. Also known as hexes, evil witches were blamed for a variety of ills and misfortunes in those times, but much of that could be avoided, it was thought, if the correct protective steps were taken. Those

5. Jared B. Ripka (born 1885), interviewed August 27, 1971 and February 2, 1974.

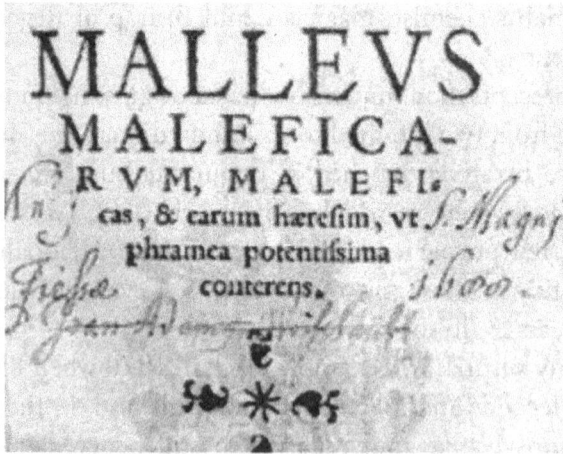

Cover of the Malleus Maleficarum. Seventh Cologne edition, 1520, University of Sydney Library

steps included something as simple as hanging a lucky horseshoe over your barn door. More often than not, however, protective measures involved engaging the services of a good witch or *braucher*—persons also sometimes referred to as "pow-wowers." Then too, there were other options to consider, including the use of ordinary pins.

"Yeah, they claim if you carry a pack of new needles you've never opened, why witches can't bother you,"[6] explained one mountaineer who had lived in an isolated central Pennsylvania farmhouse for most of his life.

He had no doubts that the old wisdom about pins was true, but his beliefs were seemingly influenced by the high mountain that towered over his homestead and turned to nothing more than dark shadows every night when the sun sank slowly behind several mountain ridges visible far in the distance to the north.[7] Moreover, not too many years prior to this and just beyond those northern ridges, there once lived folks who had similar ideas.

"If I'm hexed, I must sleep with a Bible under my pillow to keep him from working any further on me," claimed one old woman who was an exception to the rule that people who had such beliefs didn't ordinarily like to talk to strangers about them.[8]

"If I feel that I am hexed," continued the superstitious lady, "and wish to know who did it, I must take a certain unmentionable liquid [a sample

6. Ray Rowles (born 1933), recorded July 27, 1983, July 5, 1984, and May 26, 1988.

7. Ibid.

8. Myrtle Magargel, "The History of Pleasant Gap," 42nd installment of a series of articles, *Cenre Daily Times*, State College, May 19, 1936.

of her urine], put nine pins and nine needles in a vessel, and lock it in a bureau drawer that will not be used for several days. If that's done, the behexer will have to come to my place to get something, or he will burst!"[9]

Many others of her generation had similar ideas about the power of needles as a witch antidote. Down in the scenic Conodoguinet Creek country of Cumberland County, just south of where Waggoner's Gap slices through the Blue Mountain, there is an old homestead occupied by descendants of the first settlers who came here in the early 1700s.

The present owners of the house bought it in 1960, from an old couple who had lived there most of their lives. When they moved in, the new owners found evidence of just how superstitious the former owners were. In addition to placing salt under the door sills as a witch repellent, they had also, for the same purpose, hidden bottles filled with needles and pins behind the chimney. "Yeah," said the new owner, "the old people that lived here really believed in that stuff."[10]

Consequently, the further back in Pennsylvania history we go, the more fantastic the beliefs about witches and pins become. Over in Fayette County around 1786, for example, there was a scandal at the Simpson's Creek Baptist Church because the minister's wife was accused of being a witch. The accusation came from just one woman, who based it on the claim that she had watched in abject horror as the young cleric's spouse "spewed up pins."[11]

The maligned wife of the Baptist minister could perhaps be described as yet another casualty of ideas that came from the *Hexenhammer*. More accurately, she was at the least a victim of superstitious beliefs brought to the mountains of Pennsylvania from the Old World. For example, in this case there is an interesting account from England that perhaps offers some clues as to where the Fayette County accuser's ideas linking witches and pins came from.

Sandwiched between the Atlantic Ocean and the English Channel, the region known as Cornwall is one of England's most celebrated places. Noted for its legends and folktales, the Cornish peninsula was also once noted for its witch tales. Among those many tales is one about an old woman who was quite ill. Thinking she was bewitched by another woman,

9. Ibid.
10. Ray Waggoner (born 1926), recorded February 17, 1980.
11. Stevenson W. Fletcher, *Pennsylvania Agriculture and Country Life, 1640–1840*, 507.

she sought the advice of a good witch, or "Peller" as they were known in old Cornwall.

She was directed to a man who told her to procure the heart of a castrated bull and a pack of "pound pins." Then, according to the Peller, she should stick all the pins she possibly could into the bull heart. As she did so, claimed the good witch, the woman who was doing the bewitching would feel those pins "run into the bullock's heart, same as they had been run into her." The sick woman did as she was told, and soon after, affirms the tale, "the spell was taken off and the woman grew strong."[12]

But there was yet another popular tool for warding off or nullifying evil spells in days gone by, and that was the ordinary broom. Mentioned in this regard in witch stories that have appeared in previous volumes of my *Pennsylvania Fireside Tales* series, the broom holds a special place in the lore of witches and witch masters, because belief in its supernatural powers has such ancient origins. Like the horseshoe, the broom's potency was said to be derived from the Norse god Odin.

Odin, or Woden as he was known in southern Norway, fired the Teutonic peoples' imagination to such an extent that their beliefs about him formed the basis for many of their ancient superstitions. In the case of the horseshoe, for example, and in the time that might be called the dawn of storytelling among mankind, there was a belief that horses were sacred to Odin.

Arising from that belief was another—the idea that Odin had imbued horseshoes with magical strengths of their own. Similarly, based on a supposition that the broom was somehow connected to lightning, the notion arose that Odin considered the broom to be sacred as well, and so the broom was believed to have been endowed with supernatural powers too.

It was from this idea that there arose many fantastic tales about witches riding brooms and using them to conjure up storms. Likewise, it was also believed that the broom could be used against a witch if a person knew how to do so. Here in Pennsylvania, there is a tale from down in Franklin County that preserves a memory of one such episode.

Just north of Waynesboro in the scenic South Mountains of Franklin County, the small village of Tomastown sits along the western edge of Michaux State Forest. It is a picturesque region because its inherent natural beauty has been kept intact through the efforts of the state's Department of Forestry over the years.

---

12. Robert Hunt, *Popular Romances of the West of England*, 320.

Moreover, its local color has also been kept alive across numerous generations as well, because the people of the area have clung to the legends and folktales of their beloved hills; stories that have special meaning to current generations because they've been passed down to them from their ancestors. Just like the tale one Franklin County native's great aunt told to him one day, about a witch who cast a spell on her husband when they lived in Tomastown in the late 1800s.

When retelling the story, Bessie Kalamer did not say how long she had been married to Dave Mohn before he became deathly ill, but she did say she was so worried about him at the time that she thought he was going to die. He had lain in bed for several days with no sign of getting better before she finally decided to call a doctor.

The doctor prescribed some pills, but after three or four more days with still no improvement, Bessie decided to call in the services of a local "pow-wower" to "try for" her husband—that is to try to counteract any evil spells that had been cast upon him.

"So, she decided to go talk to this old lady and have him tried for, and this witchcraft woman told her that someone had put a spell on him," explained Bessie's great nephew, who heard the story from Bessie herself.

The old pow-wow doctor then performed an impressive cabalistic procedure and told her client that in order for the counter-spell to remain in effect there were certain things that must be avoided.

"If somebody comes to your house and wants to borrow something, don't give it to them!" were the directions passed on to Bessie in no uncertain terms. The cagy old woman also noted that if the person came borrowing three times and was refused each time, then the spell would be broken, at which time Bessie was to come back to her for further advice.

"So she went back home," continued Bessie's great nephew, "and she said it wasn't long 'til here this woman comes to the house and wants to borrow something! She was the woman who everyone thought was the witch who lived in the area and whose name was Grace Stauffer."

"And each time she came Bessie said, 'No, I don't have any!'"

"One time she wanted some bread, second time she wanted apple butter, and the third time she come, she didn't give her anything either. So Bess said she went back to talk to this woman.

The Rehmeyer hex house in Hex Hollow, near Winterstown, York County.

"She said, 'Now I'll tell you what to do. You go home and sweep up your rooms. Then take all the dust in the house and put it on one pile in the center of the house, and then take your broom and hit your dust pile three times and the spell will be broken.'

"She had three rooms downstairs, and she swept them all. After she did everything she was told, she hit the dirt pile three times with a broom. The third time it was like a whirlwind through the house! And she said all that dirt disappeared and her husband Dave got out of bed and asked her what she was doing. He was all right and the spell was gone!"[13]

Although it would have been interesting to ask Bessie Mohn a few direct questions about her broom experience, I'm sure she would have unwaveringly averred that everything happened exactly the way she related it to her great nephew, and that there was no question that witchcraft was

---

13. Larry Kalamer (born 1938), recorded January 25, 1998.

indeed a force to be reckoned with. At least that would seem to be a safe conclusion based on a witch tale I collected from a Centre County couple about twenty-five years ago.

The man and his wife were only in their fifties at the time, but their belief in the existence of witches and witchcraft could be traced back much further than half a century. Superstitions about such things had deep roots in both their families, their parents and grandparents passing the beliefs down to them. That is, in fact, why they were convinced that what they were telling me was something that most people would accept as indisputable truth.

"We had so hellish much trouble," explained the man, whose wife was also regaling me with the lore and tales of witches and witchcraft they had come to believe in over the years.

"Finally we went to old Bennie Ripka, and he scribbled something on a piece of paper. He said it was so witches couldn't bother the house. I put it in a Prince Albert tobacco can and put that in an old stove pipe hole there behind the chimney. It's up there yet, and if they ever tear this house down they'll find that."[14]

It was an interesting aside, but I wanted to hear the man tell me the story of how his kids were tormented by two local witches every night when the children were very young. I had heard the anecdote from someone else in this little valley in the Seven Mountains country, and he had placed the tale at this very household. Now I wanted to see if it would be corroborated by the parents who supposedly experienced the problems firsthand.

"Yeah, they seen them just as plain as could be at their bedroom window. Just as plain as I can see you," said the wife after I mentioned that I had heard something about their kids being bothered by witches.

"They kept the kids awake at night," she continued in all seriousness, "and that's how we got to know Bennie Ripka. We had to take 'em out there about three or four times."

Local braucher Bennie Ripka who lived in the nearby town of Spring Mills was called on quite frequently back in those days, and in this case, like in all his other cases, he didn't disappoint his "patients."

"He wrote something on a cigarette paper that they used to call pagent paper, or argent, or something like that. It was almost like cigarette paper," explained the wife.

---

14. Ray Rowles, Ibid.

"Yeah, he'd write—what they wrote on it, you couldn't make out what it was," chimed in her husband. "I don't know if it was in Hebrew or what. Then they'd fold that up and roll it up just like a ball and then they'd put it on a spoon with baby food and made 'em eat it. Then the kids were let go! That would straighten 'em up!"[15]

Although the parents seemed reluctant to talk about what happened after their children "were let go," my earlier teller-of-the-tale had passed on the sequel in some detail. He claimed he had heard it from the parents' father-in-law, whose name was Ira Lingle.

"They say if somebody does something like that to you and they go to the house and they get something, that'll break it right up," stated the old gentleman who believed in witches and witchcraft as strongly as the couple I was to talk to later in a follow-up interview.

He had just told us the tale of how two witches once tormented his neighbor's kids so they couldn't sleep at night, and now he was more than willing to tell us what happened when the witches came to the parent's house one day, supposedly hoping to break the counterspell that had been cast against their spell.

"Well, they set there, you know, and they had eyes that big, and they looked wild," recalled the valley native, who had known all the parties involved for most of his life.

"Then all at once the woman got up and says, 'I have to have a drink of water.'

"So she went and got it—at that time they had the water in a bucket with a dipper. She took a drink of water, and then it was all over.

"But Bennie Ripka then told Ira, 'I forgot to tell you what you should've done. What you should've told her,' said Bennie, 'You son of a bitch that won't do you no good.'

"He says, 'That would've broke it up!'"[16]

Convinced that it was a neighbor woman who had been his kids' primary tormentor, the father, when I interviewed him, still seemed to hold feelings of resentment.

"I'd like to catch her at it again sometime," said the man. "They say if you call a witch by their name followed by 'black son of a bitch,' why then

15. Ray Rowles, Ibid.
16. Randall Steiger (born 1904), recorded November 15, 1980, June 4, 1982, and May 4, 1988.

Left: Nelson Rehmeyer as a young man (from old newspaper photo.) Right: Nelson as a dapper young man (from old newspaper photo.)

they can't hurt you," he offered, noting also that he believed swearing at them like this when they're picking on somebody will "freeze them in their tracks and cause their clothes to fall off."

"Yeah," he went on, "I'd like to get her in a position like that then have everyone come around to see!"[17]

His belief about the power of foul language as a witch antidote is grounded in the mystique of witch lore as well. It was, some scholars believe, based on early Christian beliefs.[18]

Fortunately for the suspected witch of the Seven Mountains, her accuser managed to control his animosity and let her live her life in peace. It could have been a lot worse. At least the man's children weren't harmed in any manner, nor was the accused witch. That was a little different from the way a similar situation turned out, down in York County in 1929, when the "Witch of Rehmeyer Hollow" made international newspaper headlines.

On November 23rd of that year, at exactly one minute past midnight, local powwower Nelson D. Rehmeyer was bludgeoned to death by three men in his home near Winterstown. One of the assailants was himself an avowed witch who was convinced that old Rehmeyer had been the cause

17. Ray Rowles, Ibid.
18. Doctor Samuel Bayard (born 1908), recorded December 26, 1977.

of his fragile constitution for years on end, and also caused the death of his two infant sons.

Now he intended to put an end to the curse he believed the man he called "the Witch of Rehmeyer's Hollow" had placed upon him. John H. Blymire's suspicions eventually became an obsession, and his thoughts of revenge continued to work on him until he could no longer stand it. Then when his hatred boiled over, he got two accomplices to go with him to get a lock of the old man's hair. He also hoped to steal Rehmeyer's copy of Hohman's *Long Lost Friend.* Blymeir felt he needed both items to cast his counterspell, but Rehmeyer refused to cooperate, and he paid with his life.

Authorities found Rehmeyer's body two days later, and it wasn't long before the guilty parties were brought to trial for the killing. The slaying was picked up by news reporters from all over the world, who sensationalized it even more by referring to it as the "hex murder."

The publicity irked locals who resented comparisons between this trial and the infamous witch trials of Salem Massachusetts that took place in 1692. They were particularly annoyed by the reporter from the New York World who wrote that "Here in York, witchcraft is still as implicitly believed as ever it was in Salem's old days. People glance fearfully at the full moon and imagine they see a humped figure riding the birch broom across its yellow face."[19]

The trio of killers was convicted, but the story of the "Witch of Rehmeyer Hollow" lives on. Rehmeyer's house is still used as a private home, and the events surrounding his death are recalled every Halloween. On that melancholy night hayrides pass through the area to entertain those who hope to glimpse the old man's ghost. They also crane their necks, hoping to see the silhouette of that witch on a broomstick gliding across the refulgent face of a full moon.

Even though most people don't expect to see such things, the fact that the thoughts still arise is just another indication of how deeply ingrained in the popular culture those superstitions once were. Lingering fantasies like these serve as a reminder of how people thought centuries ago. On the other hand, they also may offer us an intriguing glimpse that goes further back than that. Indeed, all the way back to where witches came from in the first place—medieval minds struggling to understand Mother Nature by dressing her in a witch's garb.

---

19. Mary O. Bradley, "Haunted By the Hex," *Harrisburg Patriot News,* Tuesday, October 25, 2005.

CHAPTER 5

LOST ELDORADOS

In the 1500s they first lured the Spaniards into the Orinoco and Amazon valleys, these tales of a lost land laden with fabulous golden treasures. Then Germans caught the same gold fever and came to South and Central America as well, trekking into regions that had never been explored before. All came to search for mythical places of great riches, because legends indicated that there was more than just one such region, and their names, Cibola, Eldorado, and Quivira, fired both peoples' imaginations and their greed.

Then, over time, it also became widely believed that the discoverer of such a treasure trove would become rich, even beyond their wildest dreams. Those kinds of beliefs caused many to entertain even the slimmest of hopes that they would be the discoverer of one of these lost places of untold wealth. Hopes inspire actions, and so even the slightest of their dreams was impetus enough to bring the treasure hunter, the adventurer, and the soldier of fortune into wild and uncharted territory.

Despite the many supposed candidates, there was one in particular that fired the most imaginations. Perhaps it was because of the way its name so easily rolls off the tongue or because it was reputed to be the richest of all such sites, but it was that name that people would use when referring to any place where great wealth can be had for the merest effort. And so the name Eldorado, even today, is a name that most people recognize as a place where, for the lucky one who discovers it, treasure is there for the taking.

Here in Pennsylvania, we once had our own Eldorados, or at least that's what our legends indicate. From tales of lead deposits to stories of fabulous lodes of silver and gold that lie hidden somewhere in the secret ravines and lost valleys of our mountains, accounts like this have surfaced and resurfaced often enough over the last three-hundred years that treasure seekers have been kept busy fulltime.

It was those alluring prospects, many accounts of gold, silver, iron, and lead, which brought the first settlers into the unsettled and wildest parts of the state. Out of all those stories, however, it was oftentimes the tales of the aborigines that piqued their interest the most.

Along the Bald Eagle Mountains of Centre County, for example, local legends say it was a friendly native chieftain who first led the earliest settlers in Half Moon Valley to the great deposits of iron ore in the area known today as the Scotia Barrens. Remembered today as "the best friend the early settlers ever had," Chief Climbing Rock is said to have lived on Climbing Rock Peak, one of the foothills of the Bald Eagles, near Warriors Mark.[1]

Since no name like this appears on current topographical maps of the area, it would appear that either the peak where the old chief was once reputed to live never existed or it no longer bears his name. However, folktales preserved Climbing Rock's memory long enough that his name has come down to us today, and in that respect the old chief, if he did indeed exist, is unique in two ways.

First of all, names of Native Americans who revealed locations of great wealth to the early settlers have not often survived over time; and secondly, most of them were not as open as the Warriors Mark aborigine when it came to divulging mineral deposits of any kind to greedy pioneers.

The secretive natives as a whole reportedly liked to keep such places to themselves, and they jealously guarded the directions to their secret ore mines almost as closely as they protected their best hunting grounds. Nonetheless, during the Revolutionary War the colonists' need for lead, which was used to make musket balls for the Continental Army, reached critical levels, and lead became a much sought after commodity.

Evidence as to lead's importance to the colonial cause is, in fact, preserved in the name of one frontier fort of those times—Fort Roberdeau, more popularly known as "the lead mine fort," that was erected in Blair County in 1778 by General Daniel Roberdeau to protect workers at a nearby lead mine in Sinking Spring Valley.

1. Harry M. Williams, *The Story of Scotia*, 2.

The history of Fort Bingham in Juniata County also includes references to a lead mine in that region, but unlike the lead mine at Fort Roberdeau, the location of this Eldorado was known only to the Indian. A legend connected with the fort tells of how, "before the French War," the Native Americans of the Tuscarora Valley were on such friendly terms with the area's first settlers that they enjoyed shooting mark with them at Samuel Bingham's frontier fort.

In one version of the old tale there is an account that indicates that when they ran out of lead, the fort's visiting marksmen would excuse themselves and go off into the mountains to the north to procure more ammunition, returning several days later with exceptionally pure lead ore.

The settlers tried every ruse and means they could to get the Indians to divulge the location of their mine, but to no avail. Then they tried to find it on their own, but despite thorough searches, they were never able to find the secret deposit. That had to be a continuing source of disappointment for them, because according to one early assessment, its discovery "would have realized any man a speedy fortune in those days."[2]

A similar account is preserved in the history of Benner Township, Centre County, where it is mentioned that there was once a place here called Bald Hill, which was rumored to be the site of a well-hidden lead mine, known only to the area's Native Americans. Near this very spot, sometime before the start of the Revolutionary War, a pioneer family started clearing fields for a frontier homestead and eventually settled in the shadow of the conspicuous promontory.

Back then aborigines could still be seen at times passing through the area, and the dismal howl of the wolf and the shrill cry of the panther were not unusual nocturnal sounds, almost as common as the many trees that had to be cut down when the land was being cleared.

The task of clearing away the huge forest monarchs that had grown here for centuries was back-breaking work, but the Treaster family that did it was not cowed by the task or by the burly Native Americans who passed through the locale on occasion. The settlers were used to the sights, sounds, and tasks of those trying times, but they also had another advantage.

The Treaster men were huge specimens of humanity, known for their impressive physical strength and for their bravado, for never backing down

2. Thomas L. Montgomery, ed., *Frontier Forts of Pennsylvania—Volume I*, 591.

from a fight. That alone perhaps commanded the respect of any Native Americans with whom they came in contact. And that included those who stopped at the farm long enough to climb to the top of nearby Bald Hill and come back down with large quantities of lead ore.

Their secret treasure trove did not escape the watchful eyes of the Treasters, and they hoped to cash in on the riches themselves one day. Nevertheless, despite repeated searches, the hardy frontiersmen were never able to find the deposit. Likewise, they were never able to extract the secret as to its whereabouts from the close-mouthed miners. To the best of anyone's knowledge the ore deposits may be there yet, awaiting a discoverer.

Whether or not present-day treasure hunters would be able to find that ore, they might derive some pleasure in just visiting the old farm. For here they would be treading upon the same ground where the Treaster family sometimes observed the Cornplanter Indians crossing Treaster farmland when on their way "to see their old friend Logan."[3]

The "Logan" referred to by the historian that is quoted here would have been either the Delaware known as Chief Logan who lived for a time at Logan's Spring, now in the heart of Tyrone, Blair County, or the Mingo Chief known as James Logan who had his seat at Logan's Spring near Reedsville in Mifflin County—see the author's chapter entitled "Faces From the Past," in *Volume VI* of this series, for an interesting ghost tale related to the Chief Logan of Reedsville's spring.

Although lead deposits were one type of Eldorado that stoked peoples' imaginations here in Pennsylvania during those early times when the state was first being settled, it was the lure of silver Eldorados that fired them even more.

There were certainly enough tales of lost silver lodes in many parts of the state back then. So many, in fact, that it might not even be an exaggeration to state that whenever land speculators, surveyors, adventurers, foresters, commercial travelers, and locals sat down in taverns and stagecoach stops to rest and to socialize, the accounts were often told and retold. Along with them, there was always much speculation about exactly where the hidden deposits might be found.

From Coudersport in the Black Forest of Potter County to McConnellsburg in the South Mountains of Fulton County, and from Forest

---

3. John Blair Linn, *History of Centre and Clinton Counties*, 256.

County in the west to the legend-covered Blue Mountains in the east, there were lost silver mines aplenty—at least according to local pundits. And one thing the narratives usually had in common, was the idea that only local aborigines knew how to find these Eldorados of purest silver.

Up in Potter County, near Coudersport, pioneer landowners were once frustrated by the fact that they couldn't find the place where local Indians were getting silver ore in the mountains around Sweden Valley. Then one day in 1894 one of them came down to Coudersport by train from the Cattaraugus Reservation in New York State and stopped at McGonnell's Restaurant to eat.

From there he was seen heading out to Sweden Valley, where he walked into the woods to the south, acting like he knew exactly what path to follow. When he returned, he had some fine samples of silver ore wrapped in a bandanna, and these he freely showed to anyone in Sweden Valley who wanted to see them.

Similarly, it is recalled, he passed the samples around for inspection at McGonnell's when he got back there. Despite strong attempts to get him to reveal the source of the ore, the secretive man remained quiet and aloof, and then the next day he just walked away.

The silver samples created quite a stir in the Coudersport area, and people wondered, "How could such wealth be so near to them and yet beyond their grasp?"[4] For three years there were many who tried to find the answer to that question, but no one could claim success.

Out of ideas and options, the settlers finally hired prospector Billy O'Neill to take his divining rod and "witch" for the site in 1897. For some time, the old Civil War vet crossed and crisscrossed the fields and foothills of the area, until one summer day his divining rod bent down so strongly that he thought he had found the mother lode. Wasting no time, O'Neill went right to his employers and told them about his discovery. Shortly afterwards, a number of men with picks and shovels could be seen descending upon the locale.

It must have been quite a sight to see the excited diggers rapidly flinging shovelfuls of dirt in all directions as they excavated the area, but it must have been even more amusing to see their reaction after they had removed a huge amount of gravel and uncovered a sheet of ice. It certainly glittered

---

4. Robert R. Lyman, *Amazing Indeed*, 84–86.

like silver in the afternoon sunlight, but the glacial deposit wasn't exactly what the treasure hunters were looking for.

Thinking that the ice was left over from the previous winter, they gave up the search and went home disappointed. However, O'Neil decided to give it one more try the next summer and came back. Single-handedly the experienced miner dug through the layer of ice, and kept digging over the next several months until his shaft was thirty-two feet deep.

Despite his doggedness and no matter how far down he went, O'Neil never found traces of the silver. Eventually the project was abandoned, especially since ice kept forming on the walls of the shaft. However, the old diviner did leave a treasure of another kind behind for posterity.

To this day, the mine shaft he dug near Sweden Valley is regarded as a natural wonder, and many visitors come to see such an unusual spot. Known as the Coudersport Ice Mine, the tourist attraction still makes people think about how such a place can exist, since it does seem to defy natural laws. The oddity that makes it unique is that thick sheets of ice form on the subterranean walls in summertime, only to melt away come winter!

Then too, the mine seems to have confused men in other ways, including perhaps old Billy O'Neil. He might have thought he was divining for silver at the time his divining rod bent down with such force at this spot, but maybe he was unaware that his divining powers were limited to detecting water. Water is the substance most dowsers normally use their powers to discover, and so in this case O'Neil's powers didn't fail him after all; he did find water, even though it was in frozen form!

Similarly, frustration seems to be a common emotion for anyone who has searched for Pennsylvania's Eldorados. Imagine, for example how disappointed one Forest County pioneer must have been back in the late 1700s when he stumbled upon a cave of purest silver that he could never find again. At least that's the story the legend of this Forest County Eldorado relates.

The man supposedly lost his way in the thickly wooded hills of what is now Cornplanter State Forest near Tionesta. As night began to fall, it brought with it a fierce storm, and the tired straggler, whose last name was Hill, desperately sought a place of refuge. It was at that point that he spotted the cave.

After crawling inside he was able to light a fire, and when he did so he was amazed to see "veins of silver running everywhere in the walls and ceiling." Then as he looked around, he was even more taken aback when he spotted a large pit in the floor of the cave "filled with lumps of pure virgin silver."[5]

It is said that Hill was able to find his way back home the next morning, but after that he couldn't remember how to get back to the cave. Things apparently looked different in the light of day, and landmarks he had memorized didn't seem to be there anymore.

Nonetheless, he must have convinced himself that the vast veins of silver were not just part of a fanciful dream he might have had. After all, people in the area had known for years that aborigines were aware of such a place and had always been able to keep its exact location a carefully guarded secret.

If that thought entered Hill's mind, then perhaps suspicions crept into it as well. His disgruntled brain might have even considered the possibility that those same natives had something to do with his inability to find the cave again; that maybe, after seeing that he had stumbled upon their secret spot, they changed the lay of the land a bit to confuse any future attempts to rediscover it.

No proof of that complicity seems to have ever surfaced, but if it were true, then the Indians' efforts were entirely successful. It is said that Hill spent the rest of his life trying to find the hidden lode, as did many others, but no one was ever able to stumble upon the spot again.

About the same time, but far to the south, pioneers around McConnellsburg, in Fulton County, experienced similar frustrations when trying to find silver mines worked by aborigines in the South Mountains of that region.

It is said that many men spent years trying to find those secret mines, but once again they all came up empty-handed. They were not alone, since their failure was not unlike that of a man named Grove who searched for an Indian silver mine in western Clinton County for a good many years as well.

Around 1825, when Grove settled in the area that would later become East and West Keating Townships of Clinton County, he joined some of

5. Patrick M. Reynolds, "Cave of Silver," *Lancaster Merchandiser*, Lancaster, PA, December 5, 1979.

the first settlers to enter this wild and untamed place, including the family of Thomas Burns. The two men would later become friends, sharing the hardships and hospitality typical of the frontier. One common form of that sharing included an offer of shelter to new settlers by earlier ones who had already built their cabins.

This temporary room and board gave new settlers a chance to build their own cabins without having to live out "under the stars" where they would be subject to the vagaries of the weather or the savagery of wild animals. And so perhaps this was why Grove was staying with the Burns family when he became aware of what appeared to be a certain Eldorado near Birch Island Run.

One day during his stay at the Burns household, Grove noticed a party of Indians carrying knapsacks and other bags when heading up the West Branch of the Susquehanna. Intrigued by the odd sight, Burns couldn't get them out of his mind, and his curiosity was piqued even more when that same party returned several days later with their knapsacks and bags filled with what appeared to be rocks.

The men were invited by the Burns family to put up for the night. They accepted the invitation, leaving their bags unguarded along the side of the cabin. Then, while they were eating supper, Grove managed to sneak outside and peek into their bags. It didn't take him long to realize that the rocks were actually pieces of high-quality silver ore.

Thoughts of those rocks probably led to a sleepless night for Grove, but early the next morning after the natives had carried the silver away, he wasted no time in following their tracks back upriver in hopes of finding their secret mine. He was able to trace their footsteps all the way up to Birch Island Run, but here their tracks led into the river, and he couldn't find where they left the river on the other side.

He spent many days searching for the silver deposits, but eventually he had to admit defeat. Several years later he migrated to the west, but the thoughts of the silver samples he had seen that day in 1825 kept nagging at him until he could stand it no longer.

Bringing his son with him, Grove returned to the area and combed both sides of the river from Birch Island Run to Spruce Run without finding any trace of mineral deposits of any kind. His dreams broken, the disappointed fortune hunter went back to the west, where he would have died a forgotten man except for one geographic fact.

Settlers in the Keating area, aware of his quest, thought it appropriate to name a creek after him, and that's why the first stream north of Birch Island Run is still designated on current topographical maps as Grove Run. To this day no one has ever found the deposits that Grove so zealously sought, and which were said to be of "very superior quality."[6]

There was reportedly yet another Native American silver mine in Clinton County, that many thought contained silver ore of even finer quality than that of the Birch Island site. This notion became so popular, in fact, that more tales may have been told and retold about this mine than any other fabled mine in the state.

Although its exact location was a secret believed to be known only to local Native Americans, or so that's what most people thought, early settlers around Jersey Shore, Antes Fort, and Lock Haven were convinced that this Eldorado lay hidden somewhere on the Bald Eagle Mountain. They also were convinced that the veins of the mine were of the purest material, probably because that's what local legends seemed to indicate.

One popular tale like this recalled an incident where an old Indian once told the earliest settlers here, when referring to the mine, that "they would be shoeing their horses with silver if they knew what was on top of that mountain!"[7]

People also were fond of passing along other tales about this mine that had been passed down to them by their ancestors. One of the most common topics in many of these stories was how early pioneers who settled along the Bald Eagle Mountain would sometimes late at night see lights bobbing and weaving on the north side of the ridge. The following oral history is one such tale.

"The earliest recollection I have of the Bald Eagle silver mine, probably around 1935 or 1936, comes from my grandfather Russell Poust," explained one local man who was familiar with the old legend and who was a good storyteller besides. He had regaled us with many enjoyable folktales from the area this particular afternoon, and this was one of his most fascinating accounts yet.

---

6. Linn, Ibid, 628.
7. Mike Wheary, recorded May 6, 2002.

"Russell lived on Locust Street in Jersey Shore, and from his front porch you could look at the Bald Eagle Mountain—we call it Boat Mountain locally, which is Pine Mountain on the right-hand end or upper end and Antes Fort Mountain on the lower end," continued our storyteller.

"He would relate a story given to him by his ancestors, that in the evening after dark they would see fire flares or torches ascending the mountain. They assumed it was Indians going to the silver mine, and different times people went to investigate.

"Well, they either found nothing or they never came back! Now that's the story that was given to me as a hand down. So they either found something or didn't return, or they didn't get in the right place and came back empty-handed.

"Of course, I'd heard this story many times before a gentleman came into the store in the early 1950s. We had the hardware store in Jersey Shore at that time, and I had started my collection of Indian arrowheads before this. He come in and said, 'I wanta show you what I found yesterday!'

"I asked him where he had been, and he said they had been hunting on Pine Mountain between Aughenbaugh Gap and Pine Station. He was on a deer watch, they were putting on a drive, and he was up on a big mound of dirt so he could see. He looked down and he saw all these black things.

"He thought they were flint at the time, but when he picked them up to put them in his pocket, he noticed that they were heavy. He had picked up some arrowheads in his lifetime, so he assumed something was different here.

"Well, he had three silver-looking arrow points, which were an inch and a half to two inches long, and four or five pieces of hammered silver. They had all turned black in color, but when we touched a couple of them on the back with Brasso, behold they were silver!

"I asked him time and time again over the years to take me to where this place was, but he said he didn't think he could ever find it again. He said it was state ground."[8]

Not all Clinton County treasure hunters went away empty-handed, however. About 35 years ago, there was another Clinton Countian who did have some luck in finding an Eldorado of sorts on Short Mountain in the Pine Creek Valley. He and some friends were camping along Pine Creek at

---

8. Dave Poust (born 1930), recorded February 27, 1998 and June 21, 1998.

what was then called the Whitetail Campground when the owner of the pleasant hideaway stopped by to welcome them.

Pleasantries were exchanged and an enjoyable conversation was soon underway, which eventually turned to hunting stories and then to tales of local Native Americans. This last topic reminded the affable campground owner of a story his parents had passed on to him, and thinking his guests might enjoy the same tale, he told them all about a mysterious place on the nearby ridge.

It was an anecdote that his parents had heard from the old couple who were their neighbors when they lived along Pine Creek near the village of Waterville. Almost following in the tracks of valley pioneers, the elderly couple had moved into the area in the late 1800s, and they said they had not lived there long before an old Indian stopped by their house one day to make some inquiries.

In recalling the story, they said they thought it was about 1900 when their visitor appeared on their doorstep, but one of the things that really stuck in their minds was how old the man looked. They thought that he must have been at least ninety at that time, and from his conversation they knew he had been alive at least that long.

The wizened traveler was on a mission, and a sentimental one at that. He said he was not from the area, but that here were the mountains and valleys where his grandparents and great grandparents had once roamed, and he was anxious to explore them. He knew very little about the place and wanted to find out more about it from locals, and so he had stopped to ask some questions about prominent landmarks and the like.

In discussing the lay of the land with his new acquaintances, the man finally pointed to nearby Short Mountain and mentioned that he had once been told by his grandparents that on top of that peak there was an odd sight—a deep hole that emitted copious white clouds of what appeared to be steam.

It was a natural wonder that was enough to draw the merely curious, but the Indian said he had also been told about something else on the peak that would be even more of a lure for anyone who wanted to get rich. "If the white man knew what was in that mountain," the old man had confided to the elderly valley natives, "they would level it!"

Intrigued by the curious tale that their campground host had passed on to them, two of the weekend campers decided right then and there that they would try to find the mysterious place described in the story. They started on their quest that same day, searching only a short while before finding a path that led up the mountain directly across from their campsite.

Encouraged by their good luck and drawn by the mystery that lay before them, as well as invigorated by the beautiful sunny weather that day, the men started their climb at top speed. They made good progress for a short time, but just half a mile up the mountain they noticed that weather conditions were deteriorating rapidly.

Then, as if it came out of nowhere, a severe thunderstorm blew in, making the hikers feel almost like they had stirred the wrath of some angry god by stepping onto his private domain. Driven back by heavy winds, driving rain, and repeated lightning bolts, the adventurers had to turn around and retreat.

However, when they finally did get back down to the valley below, they found the weather there to be as sunny and pleasant as when they had started, nothing at all like the weather that had buffeted the mountain only moments before.

The eerie climactic changes left the men with an uncanny feeling, but nonetheless they vowed, since it was too late in the day that day to make another attempt for the summit, to come back the next weekend and try again.

Confident of reaching their goal this day, the enthusiasts began their climb again the following Saturday under beautiful blue skies and sunshine. But about half a mile into their trek the weather changed as abruptly as it had the previous weekend, and heaven seemed to open its faucets. Rain poured down in torrents, and by the time the deluge was over the climbers were not only soaked but also beaten back down into the valley a second time.

When they got there, they were once again greeted with beautiful weather, leaving them even more baffled and disquieted than they had been when this same thing had happened the week before. Nonetheless, they vowed that, "one way or another" they were going to go up that mountain, and they were "gonna find the hole!" So, since the day was still young, the determined sleuths turned around and started up once again.

This time the weather cooperated, and the men made it halfway up the mountain before they came to a large field of rocks. Although hard to see, it was evident that the path continued through the rocks, and so the explorers continued to forge ahead. Yet they had not gone very far when they encountered a new mystery. Here, in the middle of the rocky trail, was a pair of brand-new women's sandals, and how they came to be there caused the men some concern.

At first, they thought that a lone woman hiker had perhaps fallen and been hurt, but that left them wondering why, if that had happened, she would have taken off her sandals and left them there. It was then that they began hollering to see if anyone answered. Hearing no replies, they then fanned out and circled the area to see if she was lying unconscious somewhere. This, too, proved fruitless, and when they returned to where they had found the sandals, the shoes were still there.

Continuing up the mountain, the searchers finally reached the summit and found the steam hole, which proved to be about six to eight feet deep. Realizing that they needed more tools and equipment to explore the shaft safely and thoroughly, the successful explorers decided they would come back again on the next weekend, this time bringing along buckets and ropes. Heading back down the mountain on the same path they had followed on the way up, the excited men once again came to the rock field.

Expecting to find the sandals where they had left them, they were amazed to see that they were no longer there. When they reached the campground below, they asked everyone they could find if they had lost a pair of sandals like those that had been on the rocks above. No one had been up there, and nobody claimed to have a pair of sandals like those that had mysteriously vanished.

By this time the two adventurers were beginning to feel that they had stumbled upon one of earth's mysterious places or that someone or something was trying to steer them from their intended course of action. Despite these unsettling thoughts, the explorers were not deterred, coming back a week later with ropes, baskets, and flashlights.

When they got back up to the steam hole they began their work in earnest, with one boy staying on top to hold the rope while the other looped it under his arms and crawled down into the hole.

"There was a tiny opening at the bottom, maybe two feet; not enough to climb through," recalled the man who had been the first to lower himself into the hole in the earth.

"But I could look in, and it was quite a room. And it was pretty drafty, so there must have been another opening someplace. Nevertheless, I'd fill a bucket with rocks and Foster would pull it up and drop an empty bucket down," continued our storyteller as he explained how he and his friend took on the challenge of uncovering the mystery behind the old Indian's enticing tale.

"I'd work at this until I got tired, then I'd climb out and he'd go down and dig and send the buckets up to me. Then I'd empty them and send them back down. And then he'd get tired and come up and I'd go back down—and this was almost all day! Finally, we got an opening large enough that we could climb into it, and we turned on our flashlights and crawled in. Brilliant! It was just like there were a million lightning bugs in there! We immediately thought 'Bonanza! We've struck it rich!'"[9]

The excited men carried samples of their ore back with them that day, and later took them up to Penn State University for analysis. When the results came back, the would-be millionaires learned that they had been "fooled."

The University geologists reported that the mineral deposits were nothing more than pyrite, commonly known as fool's gold, and that the mica content far exceeded that of the gold, thereby making the rocks almost worthless from a commercial standpoint.

After reading the report, it dawned on the disappointed treasure hunters that the concentration of "lightning bugs" they had seen when they entered the cave were the specks of gold and mica that were liberally interspersed through its rock strata. Slowly and painfully it also sank in that they would have to work for a living after all. However, even though they had been fooled by the rocks, they could take some consolation in the fact that the Indians had been fooled as well, as had many others who had searched for Pennsylvania's lost Eldorados through past ages.

At least one early historian would have disagreed with that assessment, however. Sherman Day, that early compiler of numerous interesting facts on each of the state's counties, did have his reservations when writing about

9. William Tyson (born 1927), recorded April 13, 1998.

Pennsylvania's lost Eldorados and the many people who believed in their existence.

Referring to them as mostly "an auld wife's fable," he went on to note that "It is still undetermined whether such tales, which were common among the old settlers, were or were not devised by the Indians to sport with the incredulity of the whites."[10]

Taking it a step further, he went on to describe how one old aborigine, who lived along Licking Creek in Juniata County, often told the earliest settlers there about a silver mine "in a ridge near Mifflin." Nonetheless, it seems that those settlers could never find such a place, despite the fact that they often showered bribes upon the man to take them there.

This he steadfastly refused to do, probably because he was making a comfortable living by keeping its location a secret. On the other hand, Sherman Day doubted that any such place existed at all; a realization that no doubt gradually dawned on others as well over time. Hinting at possible ulterior motives, Day, writing in 1843, concluded that this Juniata County Eldorado "only produced silver for the Indian," and that "The best mines yet opened in Juniata County are on those lands that yield 25 to 30 bushels of wheat to the acre!"[11]

Similarly, over in Panther Valley, near present-day Schuylkill Haven of Schuylkill County, early settlers there were convinced that that their Native American friends had found vast deposits of gold on the Gobbleberg (a mountain near present-day Swatara.) However, just like the settlers in Juniata County who tried to find their fabled silver lode, the settlers in Schuylkill County could never find the Gobbleberg lode either.

On the other hand, in both counties the settlers who sought the treasures might have been gullible enough to be duped by the Indians. In the Juniata County case, the natives found it monetarily rewarding to perpetuate the myth of a vast lode of silver. In the Schuylkill County case, they might have just enjoyed sending their colonial friends on a wild goose chase—much like when young tenderfoot Boy Scouts are sent on a snipe hunt at Boy Scout encampments.

Pure conjecture on my part, but the tribal soothsayers' story might have been convincing enough to send fortune hunters climbing up the

---

10. Sherman Day, *Historical Collections of Pennsylvania*, 386.
11. Ibid.

Gobbleberg even under the most trying weather conditions. If so, they undoubtedly chose to endure the inclement conditions because of their gullible acceptance of the story imparted to them by those tribal elders.

The soothsayers' claim was that the gold could be found if the seeker was at the right spot at the right time, especially during a thunderstorm. It was then, so went the firmly believed tribal superstition held by the Indians, that when thunder clouds covered the mountaintop, bolts of lightning would hit the rocks, and the rocks would sometimes be "cleft in twain and the hidden recesses were discovered to be gorged with nuggets of gold."[12]

---

12. Ella Zerbey Elliott, *Blue Book of Schuylkill County*, 79–80.

CHAPTER 6

OLD SCRATCH

Ha-nis-heh-oh-nonh was the name the Iroquois gave to him—the entity they thought of as "the evil minded one" or "the tormentor."[1] To them, life without both good and evil made no sense, and so their philosophy of life included both a good creator and a bad one that were always at odds with how each accomplished his ends.

On the other hand, the "tormentor" of the medieval period was something else entirely: an evil entity not only to be feared but resisted as well, with prescribed countermeasures that included wholesale extermination of his followers (witches and wizards). So deeply engrained was the belief in the devil during those times that popular mythology even settled upon a graphic description of this fearful character.

The "ouglie devil," according to one such account, had "hornes on his head, fier in his mouth, a huge tayle in his breach, eies like basons, fangs like a boar, claws like a tiger, a skin like a bear, and a voice roaring like a lion."[2]

Such descriptions may have varied a bit from culture to culture, since there were many differences across the globe when it came to the name used to refer to the "Prince of Darkness." In the mythology of the ancient Celts, for example, he was a "hairy wood-demon" called Dus, but a similar Teutonic demon was referred to as Scrat by that ancient race; and it is from these two names that later references to the Devil were derived—namely "the Deuce" and "Old Scratch."[3]

---

1. Jesse J. Cornplanter, *Legends of the Longhouse*, 138–39, 151.
2. Charles Hardwick, *Traditions, Superstitions, and Folk-lore*, 100.
3. Ibid.

Over the centuries there were many other names that people settled upon for referring to the unpopular ruler of the underworld, with Lucifer, Beelzebub, Old Nick, and Satan among the most common ones of the lot. The Pennsylvania Germans, on the other hand, had their own unique ways of referring to the same personage. Included in their anthology was *der Mann mit em rode Wammes* (the man in the red jacket), *der Mann mit de Gloee fies* (the man with the cloven feet), and *dar Mann mit em Mischdhoke* (the man with the manure hook), the latter name derived from the belief that the manure hook was "the devil's favorite implement of torment."[4]

The idea of such an entity was a common one, but where did the idea of such a creature come from in the first place? When worldwide mythology is considered, the concept of the devil appears to be based upon a composite of many ideas, or, in the words of one noted scholar, "a grotesque compound of elements derived from all the systems of pagan mythology which Christianity superseded."[5]

If that's true, then it must have been from the Greek god Pan, a half-animal/half-human forest deity with a goat's horns and goat's hooves, that the devil got his cloven feet and his horns. And the idea that Satan could control the powers of the wind and storm came from similar ideas about the Greek God Hermes or the ancient Norse god Odin.

Little wonder then that people once held the notion that when night winds whistled through the leaves, sweeping them from their branches and causing treetops to sway and bend, it was a sign that the devil was making another midnight flight through the sky accompanied by a bevy of witches riding on their broomsticks.

Such deep-rooted fear led, of course, to many other superstitions and beliefs about the devil and his minions. To this day, for example, it is said that some Amish sects are reluctant to use hooks and eyes on their clothing because these little appendages afford a convenient place "for Satan to hang things on."[6]

Even the Nanticokes, no doubt after incorporating some of the early settlers' beliefs into their own philosophy, attributed some of nature's oddities to Satanic deviltry, referring, for example, to the wild gooseberry as the Devil's berry because of the way its berries seemingly go to waste.

---

4. Brendle, Ibid, 46, 159.
5. John Fiske, *Myths and Myth-makers*, 79, 123–25.
6. Eric Maple, *Origins: Superstitions and their Meanings*, 21.

Ripening one at a time and falling off at night, there are never enough ripe berries on the plant to be of use. Unable to understand waste like this in light of nature's other bounties, the Nanticokes could only conclude that the evil one deliberately knocked the berries off each wild gooseberry plant every night just so they could not use them.[7]

Not surprisingly, the Pennsylvania Dutchmen had a similar belief about another native plant that was once highly regarded for the medicinal qualities of its roots. Referred to by today's botanists as the Snake Root or Blazing Star, the plant was called another name by the colorful race of farmers that settled in the Blue Mountains of eastern Pennsylvania.

To them the useful posy with its bright purple florets was puzzling because of its extremely short root. They could not understand why something in which the creator had packed so many useful cures would not be larger in size. After all, extracts from this part of the plant were considered to be useful as a general tonic, a cure for sore throats, and an antidote for snake bites, as well as for numerous other maladies.

Since the root seemed to be so small in comparison to the height of the plant, which is five feet tall at maturity, the superstitious Dutchmen reasoned that the creator's good intentions must have been thwarted in some way. And to them the only entity that would have a reason for doing so was the devil himself. Then it was only a matter of time before some gifted storyteller came up with a tale that supported the prevalent belief about the plant.

We, of course, have no way of knowing today which creative teller of tales might have come up with that mythical anecdote. Nonetheless, it eventually led to the name that the Dutchmen assigned to this highly regarded plant, that was a major part of the curative pharmacopeias of that day and age.

However, the entertaining little story must have struck a chord with the mountain folks of that time, because it eventually became so engrained in their culture that it formed the basis for the name they began to use when referring to Snake Root. To them it was now *Deiwelsabbisswazel* or "the root bitten by the devil," which eventually was shortened to Devil's Bit, with the "bit" referring to the little root stub that was seemingly left behind by Satan after he decided that the number of souls entering his hellish abode was tapering off so dramatically.

---

7. Gladys Tantaquidgeon, *Folk Medicine of the Delaware*, 100.

A natural gargoyle. Taken by the author along the Loop Trail of Bear Meadows Natural Area, Centre County in 2006, this quirky image, formed by rotting vegetation, added an aura of mystery to the area for passing hikers. In my recent hikes here twenty years later, I can no longer find it.

According to this quaint yet colorful tale, the devil was so upset with the declining population of Hades he decided to investigate the matter. Eventually he found out that a certain plant was being used to counteract all the illnesses which he could inflict upon mankind. It was this little plant, he concluded, that was causing such a sharp decline in the death rate.

Enraged by the countercheck that God had used to thwart his plans, the Dark Prince tried to destroy the little plant that had become his bane, but since he could not destroy what God had created, he had to be content with biting off a large part of its root and leaving just a tiny bit behind. Since that time, concludes this little fable, all roots of the curative flower now grow only as mere stubs, grossly disproportionate to the size of the plant itself.[8]

---

8. Brendle, Ibid, 39.

Given the multitude of fears and superstitions about his satanic majesty that arose over the centuries, it's not surprising that in addition to associated plant legends there were also a number of other fairytales and folktales about him that surfaced as well. Typical of these additional legendary accounts are entertaining versions of why certain places bear the devil's name or were connected with him in some other way. One noteworthy example that falls into this category would have to be Hexenkopf Rock in southern Northampton County near, ironically enough, the village of Hellertown.

Hexenkopf, when translated from the Pennsylvania Dutch into English, means "Witches Head." Given that translation, it's not hard to guess that the early Pennsylvania Dutch families who settled near the place they called "Witches Head Rock" must have believed that this was a favorite trysting place for the devil's disciples.

And that's exactly what they did believe about this place; that it was a site where covens of witches would hold their nighttime frolics, especially on the first of May, then known as Walpurgis Night. Although this quaint belief was once widely accepted as fact throughout the countryside of eastern Pennsylvania, it was not an idea that originated there. Its origins are much older.

Living during the eighth century over in Germany, a woman named Walburga or Walpurgis became famous for her instrumental role in founding the Frankish Church, and for her leadership at the monastery of Wimborne in England. Several years after she died in 779, her body, along with her relics, was brought to the Church of the Holy Cross in Eichstatt, Germany.

Not long afterwards, it was noticed that the rock upon which her relics rested began to secrete a mysterious fluid. As time went on, it was found that the fluid seemed to possess miraculous healing powers, thereby elevating Walpurgis to sainthood. Since that time Walpurgis Night has been celebrated by the German people every first of May, the day on which her relics were brought to Eichstatt. However, that date also coincided with the date that the superstitious Franks believed witches held their annual rendezvous in the Hartz Mountains.[9]

So it seems, that it was in this manner that the witches of the Hartz Mountains, or at least, as some believe, their spirits, came with German

9. William Benton, publisher, *Encyclopedia Britannica Micropedia—Volume X*, 518.

immigrants to Pennsylvania. For there are those yet today who say that on certain nights of the year, and particularly on the night of May first, strange balls of light and dark shadows that take the form of witches in their peaked hats and long black dresses can be seen bobbing and weaving at the top of the eight-hundred-foot-high peak that is still referred to by locals as the Hexenkopf.[10]

It's not surprising then, that there are yet other locations that more explicitly include reference to the devil in their place names. For example, along the Blue Mountains of Schuylkill County between Port Clinton and Tamaqua there is a series of deep bowl-like valleys which, even at midday, seem to always be darkened by the steep peaks that frown down upon them from every side.

Because of this gloomy setting, its relative inaccessibility, and its confusing topography, there have been many tales that have arisen over the years about travelers who have lost their way when passing through here. So many in fact that people eventually referred to the place as the Devil's Hole to convey the idea that Satan himself must have created the spot as just another way to torment humankind and make life miserable.[11]

Over in the White Mountains, along the boundary line between Union and Snyder County, there is a similar place. Consisting of a deep sinkhole on the mountaintop, this gloomy site was once a favorite haunt of panthers and wolves, and so was regarded as a sinister spot to be avoided at all costs. No doubt in order to best convey this opinion to others, locals settled on a name for the place that would serve as a warning, calling it Devil's Den.[12]

Similarly, and further east near Lehigh Gap, in Lehigh County where the Lehigh River cuts through a spectacularly wild gap in the Blue Mountains, there is a massive pillar of rocks that looks to be precariously perched on the mountainside. Seemingly of unnatural origins, the first settlers there called it the Devil's Pulpit, perhaps thinking that only the devil himself would be able to scale it or have any use for it. On the other hand, it might be said that associating the devil with rocky places like this provided local storytellers with a perfect way to come up with their tales about Old Scratch.

Sitting atop many Pennsylvania ridges are places that are so rocky and remote that they would seemingly be of little use to anyone except the

---

10. Charles M. Skinner, *Myths and Legends of Our Own Land*, 85.
11. Brendle, Ibid, 90.
12. John T. Faris, *Seeing Pennsylvania*, 177.

The Sulphur Spring. The foul-smelling waters here can be found along the Loganton/ Rote Highway, Route 477, Clinton County. Early travelers must have been reminded of Satan's devilish fires when passing by this uninviting spot.

master of the underworld himself, and typical of such places are those desolate sections in the mountains where nothing can grow because the ground is thickly covered with boulders.

Although they are nothing more than products of glacial actions during the Ice Age, the boulder fields have stirred the imaginations of the tellers of tales, especially those who are fascinated by the devil and who like to portray him as nothing more than an awkward simpleton.

Typical of the Pennsylvania boulder field tales that include the devil as their primary character is a legend about a boulder-covered bare spot on Tussey Mountain near Water Street in Huntingdon County. Locals call the place the Devil's Stone Patch, saying that the boulders got there because the devil was carrying them in his apron when passing through here one day and dropped them all when something scared him![13]

A similar story is associated with the huge boulder field known as Blue Rocks on the Blue Mountain near Lenhartsville in Berks County. Scientists say these boulders are large blocks of Tuscarora Quartzite, left by glaciers that passed through here some two to three million years ago during the Pleistocene Epoch of the Ice Age. However, legend preserves a far different

13. Lawrence Bair Jr., interviewed August 29, 1972.

account as to the origins of those boulders; an account that, of course, comes from the mind of a gifted creator of fables and fairy tales.

According to the legend of the Blue Rocks, the source of the large boulders that lie here was the same source that left the rocks at the Devil's Stone Patch in Huntingdon County. In this case, however, the devil supposedly intended to put the rocks right where they are.

Those who yet recall the tale say he came through the Blue Mountains one day with malicious intentions, and anyone observing his gigantic frame as he walked along would have noticed that his hands were busy too, constantly dipping into his apron pockets to grab handfuls of special seeds, which he then let fall like raindrops upon the barren hollows and ridges of the summits below.

It was these very seeds, says the legend, which all sprouted and grew into the large rocks that still cover this area of the mountain.[14] Yet there are still more areas in Pennsylvania like this that can be mentioned also, two of the more well-known ones being Montgomery County's Devil's Potato Patch and Lycoming County's Devil's Turnip Patch.

When asked for directions to the Devil's Potato Patch, most people who live in Ridge Valley, near Tylersport in Montgomery County, can provide them, but the number of those same folks who know how the unusual spot got its name are decreasing every year.

The bed of large round boulders that covers a section of the hills beside Ridge Valley Creek are so weather-beaten that it's obvious the stones have been there for countless generations, and so it's probably not surprising, after so many years and with the decline in the popularity of storytelling as a form of entertainment in the mountains, that those who know the legend have dwindled rapidly, too, as time marches on.

Nonetheless, there are many who are always fascinated by such stories, even though the accounts are nothing more than fairytales. Consequently, it's because of folks like them that the fable of the Devil's Potato Patch has managed to survive.

According to some versions of the little account, the devil took a sudden interest in potatoes one day when one of his henchmen informed him that they were very good to eat. He had never heard of these treats before and so didn't even know what they looked like, except that they were round

---

14. Grant N. Sassaman, ed., *Pennsylvania, A Guide to the Keystone State*, 383.

and hard and that there were many objects like that in an area of the upper world that is now called Ridge Valley.

Without a second thought, the devil set off in a rush to lay up a store for himself, and when he arrived in the valley, he was gratified to see that there were indeed many of the hard round objects here that he had been told about.

Immediately he began to collect as many of them as he could, and soon he had a large pile that covered an acre or more in size. However, once he realized that his potatoes were not the real thing, he left as quickly as he had come, and his collection of boulders remains there to this day, a reminder of one of Satan's rare visits to the earth's surface regions.[15]

Yet another tale like this is told about a large collection of boulders along Route 15 on the Bald Eagle Mountain above Williamsport in Lycoming County. Although all the rocks are a grayish color today, geologists say that back in pioneer days the sandstone boulders here were mostly all white. However, interspersed among the others were a few stones that were of a reddish or purple hue, which tended to stand out among their pale companions.

To some settlers the colorful palette conjured up images of turnips growing in a garden, and perhaps it was that step in thinking that led some storytellers to invent a tale about how these "turnips" were actually remnants of one other time when the devil visited the earth's surface.

This time, according to the Lycoming County tale, which is apparently based upon an anecdote popularized by Henry Shoemaker (which makes the story's origins suspect right away, since Shoemaker is known to have invented many of the stories he presented as real folktales), Old Scratch came to the boulder field on Bald Eagle Mountain because he was looking for a way to make some easy money. He had been told that turnips were easy to grow on a spot like this and were also easy to sell. However, despite his best efforts, the devil could not clear away enough rocks to plant more than just a few of his turnip seeds, and so abandoned his project.

Regardless of the apocryphal origins of the tale or who invented it, it was perhaps the reason why the area's residents settled on Devil's Turnip Patch as the name they used to refer to this particular boulder field. On the other hand, maybe someone first invented the name, and a clever storyteller came up with an anecdote to go with it.

---

15. Brendle, Ibid, 92.

Either way, the legend about the devil and his turnips became so popular that it was accepted as a welcome addition to the colorful sagas of the area, and it certainly seemed to fit in well with the color scheme of the rocks.

Some versions of the story may have even claimed at one time that the turnip-colored boulders lining the boulder field were what the devil actually produced when he tried to grow the real thing. However, regardless of how it got its name, the place became the Devil's Turnip Patch, and so it remains today.[16]

Certainly, episodes about the devil's emergence from the underworld to sample life on earth are entertaining and colorful, but they are not frightening in any way, and that seems odd. For one thing, it's likely that a storyteller's purpose in telling devil tales was to frighten listeners out of their wits by trying to convey the terror that someone might feel if they did come face-to-face with the evil one. The best way to instigate that kind of fear, they no doubt realized, would be to tell the story as though it actually happened. That's why, I would suggest, that there are so many accounts of people meeting the devil up-close and personal. One of the best examples of that motif, and one of my favorites, is a tale I like to call "the Devil at the Crosslane."

The story of the Devil at the Crosslane was one of the first anecdotes I collected when I started gathering such stories back in 1970, and I can still picture in my mind the gaunt, grey-haired old lumberman telling us about this unusual episode while sitting there in his comfortable rocking chair.

The account, he claimed, after taking a satisfying puff on his pipe, was told to him by the two men who had the devilish experience one night when they were returning home in a horse-drawn buggy, after attending a local dance somewhere in the Seven Mountains country of Centre County.

"When I left Decker Valley in 1904," began our eighty-six-year-old raconteur, "I came into Georges Valley to work for a man named Jim Reeder. I wasn't there too long until I met John Faust. The thing I remember most about him was that he was a big husky fella who would pick a fight with anybody, no matter what his size! He was as rough as anyone and afraid of no one! That's why I was surprised when he and his cousin

---

16. Abby J. Porter, "That Rocky Area is the Devil's Turnip Patch," *Williamsport Sun-Gazette*, October 12, 1997.

Elmer each came up to me at different times and told me about their devil scare."[17]

According to the Faust boys' account as it was told to our storyteller back in 1904, the cousins, one night a number of years prior to that, had dates for a big dance being held somewhere in the area. The young blades, in their horse and buggy, picked up their girls in Potters Mills and made an uneventful trip to the shindig.

The events of that night went smoothly, as did the return trip from the festivities, but the same could not be said of the trip home after the Fausts dropped off their young ladies back at General Potters' hamlet.

It so happened that the horse pulling the boys' buggy that night was a spunky little mare they called "Kickin' Kate." They had decided upon that name because when the horse was in one of her mean moods she would often kick back viciously with her rear feet, knocking down anything that happened to be behind her.

On this night, however, traveling down the Lower Georges Valley Road, little Kate lost her spunk altogether as she came up beside the first gap in the mountains. Here, near a road dubbed by locals as the Crosslane, the usually frisky animal stopped dead in her tracks, and neither John nor Elmer could get her to start again.

Referred to as the Crosslane because it allowed the traveler to cross over the valley from the Lower Georges Valley Road in the south to the Upper Georges Valley Road to the north, the passage was nothing more than a dirt road at that time. It usually was a well-used route, as evidenced by the fact that the Crosslane Schoolhouse stood along the byway back then, but on this particular night and at this late hour there seemed to be no other horses or buggies out and about.

The lack of human activity certainly would have made the night seem less friendly, and that, coupled with the fact that their horse appeared to be scared of something, must have caused the men some uneasiness. They may have tried to rationalize Kate's behavior by thinking that she was frightened by a snake on the road. On the other hand, it would not have seemed likely to these country lads that a snake would be lying on the road at that time of night.

Other thoughts may have entered into their heads as well, but none of them could have prepared the men for what they saw when they looked

---

17. Jared B. Ripka (born 1885), interviewed August 27, 1971 and February 2, 1974.

View of the Rocks at Hexenkopf Rocks. Weird tales still cling to this strange spot that some even today say is still haunted by ghosts of witches from the olden time that hold their witches' frolics here to pay tribute to Old Scratch, who they worship as their lord and master.

over to the road bank on their right. Sitting there, with his arms resting on his knees and his head propped up in his hands was what, at first glance, appeared to be a man.

As the burly country lads continued to gaze upon the strange figure, they became more and more unnerved, particularly since he offered no greeting and just sat there motionless, staring down at them with a malevolent glare.

Just then, the dark clouds that had been blocking the face of the moon were swept away by a blast of wind, and pale beams of moonlight lit up the hillside. It might be said that the darkness of that night, coupled with the unexpected appearance of anyone at that place on the lonely road, were enough to scare the horse and shift the men's imaginations into overdrive, but they both would later swear that when the moon's silver rays fell upon the dark shape, they could see horns on its head!

With the horrible figure right next to them, both men frantically tried to get Kate to move, but all their actions and coaxing were in vain. Then, just when the Fausts were ready to jump off their buggy and flee for their very lives, the black figure on the bank stood up and walked away.

The sight of the retreating shape seemed to calm the little horse; Kate started off on a gallop right after the horrifying hallucination or delusion melted into the pitch-black woods of the nearby mountain. On the other hand, the figure's disappearance did not exactly calm the young men. Both would later swear that when they looked at the thing's feet as it walked away, they were horrified to see hooves like "cow's feet" where human ones should have been.

To their dying day both John and Elmer Faust, when talking about the figure they saw that evening, swore that they "had never seen anything like it," but Elmer always seemed to have the last word on the matter. Referring to John's normally pugilistic tendencies, Elmer would laugh and say that on that particular night even John decided that flight was probably better than fight. On the other hand, perhaps the odd creature, if there was one, was scared off that night as well.

It seems no one here has reported seeing anything like that again, but over the years even evidence of the Crosslane Schoolhouse has disappeared, and more houses line the once-lonely lane which today isn't even referred to as the Crosslane by locals anymore.[18]

The old byway so appreciated by the valley's first pioneers, is now a paved one and has been named Reeder Road. But changes like this don't necessarily mean that *der mit de Gloee fies* (the man with the cloven feet) will not be seen around here again sometime.

On some dark and somber night, when the night winds are strong enough to bend the treetops and cause dark clouds to whisk across the face of the full moon, the gargoyle-like image might appear at the old Crosslane once again, but only if he's had his fill of scaring people in other places.

Accounts of episodes like the Fausts' have surfaced in other parts of the state as well, and so Old Scratch does seem to move around. Or at least two other legendary narratives seem to indicate that's the case: one from Clinton County and one from Franklin County, with the Clinton County tale recalled to us by another octogenarian one summer day in 1999 at the quaint mountain village of Loganton.

---

18. Ripka, Ibid.

"My mother's aunt used to come here and tell ghost stories," began our interesting narrator, who seemed to be somewhat of an authority on 'things that go bump in the night.' "I used to be afraid to go to bed at night," he continued, recalling some of the scariest tales his aunt would relate to him.

"She told the story about the fella going down through The Narrows in a buggy. That's the old road going to Lock Haven—around the curves, you know. I don't know what the route number is, but it goes back through the mountains to Rote.

"At that time, they'd have lanterns sittin' in with them. Well as he was goin' through the Narrows there, he was startled when he suddenly realized there was something sittin' alongside of him. This figure apparently just appeared out of nowhere, and when he took a closer look at it, he could see in the lantern light that it had hooves where its feet should have been!"[19]

No further details about this weird tale were forthcoming from our host. Too much time had passed since those days, and those who perhaps could have supplied more information had died long ago. So we will, of course, never know exactly what happened there along the Loganton/Rote highway; what events took place that led to this weird tale. It is interesting, of course, to speculate what may have happened, and, as in many of these accounts, it might have been nothing more than an imagination run wild.

The old road to Rote appears to be Route 477 today. It runs over Big Mountain from Loganton and eventually down into the small village of Rote in Nittany Valley, Clinton County. Sitting beside the road, just outside of Loganton, is a pavilion with a sign on it that denotes the "Sulphur Spring."

The pavilion covers a cistern which holds the sulfurous waters that have bubbled up here since time immemorial. However, back in horse and buggy days the sulfur spring was probably not covered, and, if not, its foul-smelling odors would have been easily detected by any passersby.

A particularly timid or easily frightened person, traveling along this lonely road on a stormy night, could have gotten a whiff of the spring, which, in combination with the other stimuli, might have been enough to excite his imagination. At that point, images of Hades and its dark chambers could have come to mind next.

After all, wasn't Hades filled with sulfurous vapors? At least some accounts of those days would have led one to believe so. From there it

---

19. George Tibbens (born 1913), recorded July 10, 1999 and July 25, 1999.

would have been an easy step to imagine that the devil himself couldn't be that far away if the fumes of hell were that strong!

Although details about this devilish encounter no longer remained in the memory banks of our interesting storyteller, his little tale, coupled with the Faust story, did indicate that the account was one that liked to move around. It was a theory that seemed to be confirmed when I recalled that I had heard another storyteller relate a similar tale to me down in Franklin County the year before.

"One of my grandfather's cousins was Nelson Kalamer, and this was a story he used to tell," was the way the Franklin County man began one of the many old-time episodes from the South Mountains he would tell us this day.

Nelson Kalamer's devil tale never varied when he told it, and it certainly left a lasting impression upon our storyteller. According to him, Nelson's weird encounter occurred around 1920 when he was driving his horse and buggy along the Old Forge Road near Glen Forney, Franklin County. He was intending to go into Waynesboro that day, but his trip was rudely interrupted by something that sent shudders up and down his spine, and would do so again whenever he recalled the event to people afterwards.

"He said he got about a mile down the road from where he lived," continued Kalamer's distant cousin, "and the horses stopped. The horses wouldn't go, and so he took a whip and whipped them to try to get them to go, and they wouldn't. He looked to see what was there because he thought there was a snake that scared them and made them stop. But when he stood up in the wagon to get a better look, there was the devil sittin' in the middle of the road! Well, it scared him so bad he said he turned the horses around and came back!"[20]

Much to our pleasure, this account reminded our Franklin County source of yet another devil tale, one that happened to his grandfather one night in 1900. At that time his grandfather, who was born in 1869, lived near the Franklin County village of Old Forge and worked for the Mount Alto Iron Company near Tomastown.

He traveled to work every day, a distance of about eight miles, in his horse and buggy. It was not an easy life, between the hard work and poor pay at the iron company, coupled with his long daily commutes, and so

20. Larry Kalamer (born 1938), recorded January 25, 1998.

sometimes on weekends he would, according to his grandson, "take off in the horse and wagon and go get drunk."

Eventually the hard drinking must have taken its toll on the ironworker, because one night when he came back from a night on the town, he didn't put the horse and buggy in the barn like he usually did. Instead, he asked his wife to do so. Although somewhat surprised by the request, she went out to the barn, where yet another surprise was waiting.

The first thing Mrs. Kalamer noticed when she looked at the young mare was how "lathered up" it was; a sure sign it had been driven hard. She quickly unharnessed the poor animal from the wagon and bedded the horse down for the night. But her curiosity had been piqued.

"What was you runnin' the horse for?" she asked her husband when she got back to the house, but her question was answered by another.

"Is the man still sittin' in the seat?" was her spouse's anxious reply.

"There was nobody in the wagon that I seen," huffed the irritated wife, who then accused her vagrant spouse of "seeing things." Taken aback by her accusation, the chastised husband felt obligated to explain himself.

"He said somebody got in the wagon with him," recalled the grandson of the man who had to explain to his wife what he had seen that awful night over a hundred years ago. "He said as he was coming home, the devil climbed in the wagon with him! He said he kept getting closer and closer to him until he was sittin' right next to him, and he was so hot he purt near set him on fire! He was that hot that he thought it was the devil that climbed in the wagon and rode home with him!"

Needless to say, the man's wife didn't buy his story. Calling him an "old fool," she said he was imagining that horrible things were after him because he had a guilty conscience about his weekend binges. However, the man's grandson had a different explanation about his grandfather's claim that the devil had jumped into his wagon with him. To the grandson it seemed reasonable to note that heavy drinkers sometimes get to a point where their brains are so besotted by alcohol that they begin to have hallucinations. Today we call those alcohol-induced hallucinations the DT's or *delirium tremens* but in those days they had a different name.

"He must have gotten the 'snakes', what they called 'the snakes',"[21] concluded our storyteller in his attempt to come up with a rational explanation for this grandfather's strange experience. It seemed as good an explanation

---

21. Ibid.

The Devil's Turnip Patch. Along Route 15 on the Bald Eagle Mountain above Williamsport in Lycoming County, its many purplish stones once reminded storytellers of turnips, and hence the legend that still clings to this colorful boulder field.

as any, considering the alternatives, and so that's probably how people left it in those days. Nonetheless, even though reasonable rationalizations for these supposed devil encounters sometimes prevailed, there were always those who preferred to believe in many of the old-time beliefs about the devil and his minions.

And so the superstitions held on for many years, even right down to the present age, which meant I could hear some of them directly from the mouths of old folks who, when young, had heard the same beliefs from the old folks of their day. There were many uncanny ideas, like the devil having his own version of the Bible ("a black book with hair all over it"[22]), and that certain folks really knew how to literally raise the devil.

And as far as this last idea, there was once a man over in Clearfield County who, in some locals' minds, fit into this category perfectly. It is, of course, a highly exaggerated tale, but one clearly designed to strike fear into a storyteller's audience.

22. Roy Funk (born 1923), interviewed January 13, 1997, recorded January 22, 1997.

Up in the wooded heights called Punkin Ridge, in Chest Township of Clearfield County, during the 1930s, there was an ancient homestead that was always avoided by those who lived within fifty miles of the ramshackle place. Although the appearance of the house alone would have been enough to signal passersby that they were not welcome there, it was the reputation of the house's owner that struck the most fear into the hearts of anyone who knew about his special powers. For here, quite a few believed, lived a man who was possessed by the devil.

Shunned by all wildlife in the daytime, the old place only seemed to come to life as night fell. And when the cloak of darkness was complete, it seemed to draw out rats, bats, and screech owls, all of which cast a decidedly ominous aspect over the shadowy clearing where the structure stood. At such times, said many who claimed to have seen it themselves, the house's lonely inhabitant would stir from his daytime slumbers and begin his nightly proceedings.

And those who were brave enough to spy on him said those proceedings were something to behold. Not only could he make chairs dance, they professed, but he also could "conjure up dancing snakes and piglets" from the fire in his fireplace or from his kitchen stove. However, the most damning evidence about the old codger who lived within these dark walls came from those who had secretly followed him from his house to a nearby intersection one night when the moon was full.

On that night, so the spies claimed, the man took a black cat with him and at exactly midnight buried it alive in the middle of the crossroads. So frightening was the episode that not one of the concealed onlookers was brave enough to stay around to see what happened next. Scattering like feathers in the wind, the heretofore fearless snoops high-tailed it back to the safety of their mountain homes.

No doubt those present that night forgot to mention their unceremonious departure when telling their friends about the strange proceedings they had witnessed, but the rest of their story would have been enough to send shivers up the spines of anyone hearing it. The reason for this reaction, and the reason for the men's untimely retreat, was that the ceremony performed by the old man that night followed the procedures that many in those days believed were used by wizards who had the power to conjure up the devil to do their bidding.

No doubt the poor old man was mentally ill. He must have suffered from delusions, while his neighbors, ignorant of the vagaries of the human mind, could only attribute his strange behavior to supernatural causes. It was for this reason that they also believed that when the man was dying, he claimed that "the devil was in the room, waiting to take him away!"[23]

Given such beliefs and tales, it's no wonder that many folks were quaking in their boots when, in 1909, the Jersey Devil scare swept through New Jersey and into central Pennsylvania. Known also as the Leeds Devil, named from the Pine Barrens family into which it was said to have been born, the Jersey Devil created quite a stir during the first two months of 1909.

Many sightings were reported of this "flying serpent" which, according to one account, had "the head of a dog, the face of a horse, the wings of a bat, the feet of a pig, and a forked tail!"[24]

Still unexplained, except for those who attribute them to a rash of mass hysteria, many of the Jersey Devil sightings remain a mystery to this day. Since some believe the beast still lurks in the dark pine forests of southern New Jersey, the possibility of meeting it deters the faint-hearted from penetrating too far into the New Jersey pine lands, even to this day. So, it's not hard to imagine how much fear the thought of encountering it must have generated back in 1909, even as far west as Pennsylvania's heartland.

Back about that time, there was a young farm boy who lived on his family's farm near the small village of Tusseyville, in Centre County. One of the lad's nightly chores before going to bed was to walk out to a nearby spring to fill water buckets for the next day's household use.

However, on this particular night the twelve-year-old was scared, even though his dog Bill was with him. The boy had been hearing stories about the so-called Jersey Devil for several days, and now he was afraid it might swoop down on him that night.

Ignoring his apprehensions, the water boy was able to get to the spring, get his buckets filled, and get back to the house safely. However, when he went into the house, he also let his pet come in with him. The happy canine curled up in a cozy corner and prepared to sleep in comfort, but when the lady of the house saw the animal, she was not amused.

---

23. Author unknown, "Clearfield County Tale Claims Man Could Summon Devil," *The Centre Daily Times*, October, 1997.
24. James F. McCloy and Ray Miller Jr., *The Jersey Devil*, 23ff, 20, 54, 101ff.

"Now Earl, you know that that dog isn't allowed in the house," exclaimed the housewife as she admonished her son.

"I know," replied the sheepish young man, "but I told him if he wouldn't let that Jersey Devil get me when I went for water, he could sleep inside tonight!"

According to my grandfather's sisters, who passed this story on to me, the Frazier's dog Bill did sleep inside that night, and my grandfather took the dog with him to fetch water every night after that because he wanted to have some protection against "that Jersey Devil" which seemed to be terrorizing the countryside.[25]

---

25. Ida Frazier and Harriet Frazier, recorded September 17, 1989.

CHAPTER 7

NO PLACE LIKE HOME

Those who love a locale because they were born and raised there, or because their ancestral roots forever link them to it, will come to realize at some point that the history of that area and its longtime residents have a special connection. Local landmarks and names of any families that have ever resided within the boundaries of their familiar home territory seem to be permanently stamped upon the aboriginal mind.

And time seems to stand still in such places as well, almost as though nothing ever changes as years go by. At least that's an impression many might get when they hear natives using the names of previous owners rather than those of present owners when referring to houses and farms that have stood there for well over a hundred years.

"Turn right at the old Smith place," or "Take the first left after the Baker farm," might be the way an elderly resident of the area would give directions to some other local person, even though there hasn't been a Smith or a Baker living at either homestead for at least three generations. So, it would seem that people are reluctant to let go of their placenames, in the same way that ghosts seem reluctant to leave a place on which their images and essences are indelibly impressed.

It could be argued that any house in which people once lived and died is haunted in one way or another, just because no family can go through life without experiencing its giddy highs and its rock-bottom lows. And extreme passions like these, say some parapsychologists, are forever imbedded upon the fabric of space and time itself as visual images which can

Homans' Store. Potters Mills, Centre County.

sometimes reappear as "ghosts" to those who have the gift the Scots once called "second sight."[1]

Then one has to wonder, why isn't every house a haunted house? Why can't those who have the faculty of being able to see ghosts, see them everywhere? The answer, I think, if you grant that such things are possible, lies in the fact that it takes a special set of circumstances to reach a critical mass; a point at which the effects become most evident. And most prominent among those ingredients, it would seem, is the manner in which the ghost, when in human form, lived and died. Nonetheless, despite the fine balance it might take for ghosts to materialize, the phenomenon is a long-lived and world-wide one.

There is no doubt, since it is so well documented, that mankind has harbored a belief in ghosts throughout recorded history; to the point where such beliefs even controlled some people's lives. Over in the British Isles, for example, it is said that many Brits once felt it was not safe to go outside between the hours of midnight and the sound of the rooster's crow because they believed that was the time period when spirits, both good and evil, could, and did, visit the earth.[2]

1. John Ingram, *The Haunted Homes*, 167.
2. J. A. Brooks, *Ghosts and Legends of Wales*, 16.

Today those spirits are still visiting us, or at least that's one possible conclusion that can be reached if any research is done on the matter. Haunted houses apparently still abound, as do haunted cemeteries and spirit-filled woodland glens, and such places are not for the faint-of-heart.

Readers of the *Pennsylvania Fireside Tales* series have been entertained by many tales about places like this, and the paragraphs that follow in this chapter present one more haunted house. It is a building that, even though it sits at a busy gateway to some of the airiest and prettiest mountain scenery in the state, harbors a dark secret whose roots may lie in a forgotten burial ground atop a nearby mountain peak.

At the intersection of Routes 322 and 144, in Potter Township of Centre County, there is a quaint country store in the village of Potters Mills that is a favorite stopping place for motorists as they enter or leave the Seven Mountains country. Perhaps it's the location that draws the passersby, who see the gas pumps and decide that they'd better fill 'er up before heading to wherever they're going.

Or maybe it's the old-time look of the structure that invokes a nostalgic chord in the minds of travelers, thereby drawing them in for a closer look. Regardless of whatever the case may be, there's a good possibility that the store would attract even more visitors if its ghostly inhabitants were inclined to be more sociable.

"We both kinda wished we had seen the spirits," said the old store's current owner, as she recalled how she and her husband sometimes heard ghostly footsteps in the upstairs apartment, after they first bought the building and spent late hours working in the store area on the first floor.

"When you first move, everything is in disarray," stated the young woman who was not at all reluctant to share her strange tale with us. Her story started from the day she and her husband moved into the apartment above the store they had recently purchased. It was early in the fall of 1996, and they had not yet had time to put everything in its place.

"So we had done all our bed linens and such, and just thrown them on a chair, thinking we'd fold them the next night," she recalled. "So we were workin' late hours, but when we came home Bruce said to me, 'Thank you for folding those bed linens!'

"And I said, 'I was going to thank you for folding the bed linens!'

"Well, right away we knew we had a ghost, and that it was a very friendly ghost; one that we could easily live with. We had had a ghost in another home in Bellefonte, so it was something we both recognized.

"There was just the two of us living there at the store, but we'd sometimes hear someone running back and forth, back and forth, upstairs, when we'd be working in the store downstairs. Then a couple weeks after we'd moved in, the people who had lived there before us came into the store, and we asked them if they had any ghosts upstairs.

"They both kinda chuckled and then said, 'We wondered if you would figure it out or find out about it!' She apparently had the ability to see them, because according to her there were four spirits, that of a little girl, her mother, her father, and her little dog, and that the running back and forth would be the sound of the little girl playing with her dog!"[3]

Intrigued by this exciting news, the new owners asked the former tenants for more information, but the woman said she could not tell them much more than she had already. She had not recognized any of the ghosts, even though the spirit of the little girl, for some strange reason, kept appearing and reappearing to her. This, of course, had piqued her curiosity, causing her to wonder who the little waif may have been and what fateful events might have locked the girl's spirit to this remote spot.

Then, almost as though the playful sprite had led her to the right place and time, she found herself, on another day, looking at an old-time picture someone was passing around at a family reunion. The photo was a group photo of some of her ancestors, but there among those long-dead relatives was the face of the little girl! Somehow, the woman realized, she must be related; and that conviction became stronger when it suddenly dawned on her that the face in the picture bore an eerie resemblance to the face of her own daughter!

The former tenant said that things then got decidedly scarier after that, when one day she went downstairs to the store's basement storage room to get something. Once down there she felt compelled to look out one of the basement windows, and as she did so she saw, standing just outside and looking as normal as real people, the little girl and her parents.

At first, she wanted to look at the spectral trio to see what they might be doing, but then they started to motion to her to come through the

3. Brenda Homan, recorded June 8, 2006.

window and join them. Deciding that it would not be a smart thing to do, the unnerved onlooker turned around and went back upstairs. It wasn't long afterwards that she and her husband decided to move out.

The young woman's spine-tingling encounter with ghosts while in the store's basement storage room was not the first supernatural event, nor the eeriest anyone had ever experienced in the store. Some twenty years prior to that, another younger woman had her own personal journey into that otherworldly land some have referred to as the twilight zone—a place where our wildest dreams become reality and our deepest fears reduce us to such a state of helplessness that we become trapped in our own nightmare.

This earlier ghostly episode occurred around 1946 when the little country mercantile, complete with its pot-bellied stove, spittoons, and

Haunted House on the Hill. Another example of an old house that's reputed to be haunted, this place on the outskirts of Millheim in Centre County is reported to be home to a number of spirits, including a man in carpenter's overalls who crawls around the bed of sleeping occupants on his hands and knees; a luminescent image of someone hanging with a rope around their neck in the upstairs hall; and another spirit who likes the sound of running water. Currently uninhabited, it seems that it's a hard place to rent. People who decide to stay there don't seem to hang around very long, because, say locals, it's just too haunted.

complimentary bench for the old-timers who often came to loaf and chew tobacco, was sold to the Johnsons. Shortly afterwards the new owners engaged in an extensive remodeling program, eventually moving into an upstairs apartment above the store. It was to this upper floor that the family would retire after closing the place at the end of the day.

"Well, he had closed the store this one particular night," recalled the store owner's daughter, who was about six years old at the time of the incident. "And he asked me to go downstairs into the store to get some sort of food. I had never been frightened or felt anything before this, and so I went down the stairs and turned right, into the feed room; it was a room where we kept cattle feed we sold to farmers back then, but that night it was empty. Anyhow, when I went into that room, all of a sudden it lit up like someone had turned on the lights!"

It was an unnerving moment for the young girl. Her father, as part of his remodeling efforts, had, except for those on a set of French doors, painted all the room's windows shut with a dark green paint "so people couldn't look in." In addition, on that night the dreary gloom of a late winter evening had descended upon the valley; and that, coupled with the fact that the store owner's daughter had not turned on the electric lights in the cheerless room when she first entered, meant the room was not well lit when she stepped into it.

However, even though she was unnerved by the sudden illumination that occurred as she passed through the doorway, what appeared in that unearthly light was enough to take her breath away; an unfortunate scene that might have been taken right out of a novel like Harriet Beecher Stowe's *Uncle Tom's Cabin*.

At first glance the images were too faint for the surprised store owner's daughter to realize what she was looking at. Then slowly but inexorably, a cold and clammy sensation of fear began to overwhelm her as the shadowy shapes gradually materialized into more discernable forms. Then after the scene became completely distinct, she could see the people in it. It was such a vivid image that to this day she can still describe the clothes they were wearing and the expressions on their faces.

Describing them as "colored," a term used in a non-derogatory way in those days, our narrator explained that standing there before her was what appeared to be a Black family: a man, a woman, and a child.

"They were all looking up," she recalled, "and when I looked up," she continued, "I saw a colored boy there; and he was hanging by the neck!

"I could see the rope," explained the woman whose encounter with the old store's ghosts was something she has never forgotten, "and I just remember his mouth being open and his tongue hanging out. He was barefooted, had a white shirt on, and he had dark pants on like knickers.

"I had never seen knickers before, but later I realized his pants must just have been hand-me-downs that were too short because they were several sizes too small for him. I would guess he was about twelve years old, and he wasn't real tall.

"And immediately when I saw that, I saw his mother, I presume it was his mother, sobbing and crying. She was heavy—a fat woman. And she had a dark-colored dress on with some white. She also was wearing a bandanna of some sort around her head. And there was another child, a smaller boy, and he was hanging on her dress, crying because she was crying. The man had long pants on, and maybe his feet were bare, but he was, like, stunned."

Not wishing to linger near this tragic picture, the horrified onlooker finally rushed out of the room where she had seen the images of the family. It perhaps was a scene that had been indelibly stamped on this particular fabric of space-time at the moment the event took place, and perhaps it had been replayed here many times afterwards.

Whatever the case may be, apparently no one had noticed it before, until this night when the store owner's daughter happened to be there to witness it. However, she could not convince her parents that she had seen something unusual.

"They just laughed and thought it was hilarious," explained the woman who was telling us about her ghostly experience. She, on the other hand, didn't think there was anything funny about it, at least not in a humorous way.

"After that," she continued, "I always had a funny feeling whenever I'd go down into that room, and whenever Dad would tell me to go down, I would bribe my sister or brother to go down for me!"[4]

It seems, however, that her siblings never saw anything unusual in the feed room when they ventured into it late at night, and no one has reported seeing the family's suicide scene in recent years either. So perhaps the ghosts

4. Vivan Johnson Stover, recorded January 10, 2006.

were laid at last on that eventful night some sixty years ago when their terrible vigil unfolded before the eyes of the storekeeper's daughter. On the other hand, perhaps it was another, more recent, event that quieted the restless spirits once and for all.

It took over a hundred and fifty years for this hiding place, a spot that might well be called a last refuge, to be discovered by local historians, but thanks to the unlikely combination of modern technology and a nineteenth century map, the forgotten forest sanctuary that may hide the remains of the Black family of Homan's Store appears to have been uncovered at last.

There are those who might claim otherwise; might contend that the spot is not a final resting place. Nonetheless, even today anyone who enjoys a good mystery can conduct their own investigation into the matter if they so desire. All it takes is a copy of that old map, and a desire to take a nostalgic trip into the past.

Collectively known as Pomeroy's Atlas of Centre County, the cartographic views contained in the set of 1874 township maps afford an interesting and pleasurable view of what those areas looked like shortly after the Civil War. Locations of houses, stores, mills, churches, and cemeteries are shown quite clearly on the layouts, along with names of the owners of the different establishments.

The old names are a link to the long ago, evoking pleasant familial feelings in those who recognize them as titles belonging to their own ancestors or to families their grandparents used to mention when reminiscing about the past. Then, too, there is the urge to take a metal detector to those locations where it's indicated that a blacksmith shop, school, church, or lumber mill once stood; just to see if there are any artifacts of those places left today.

Likewise, the many locations marked as cemeteries on the old layouts are a lure to those who are interested in seeing some of those timeworn burial grounds and the tombstones they hold. However, in the case of the little "God's half-acre" on First Mountain, there are no tombstones that mark the final resting places of those who were interred there.

It is an unusual spot, this quiet place of final rest along what was once the busy thoroughfare called the Old Lewistown Pike. Merely abbreviated as "cem" on the Potter Township map in Pomeroy's Atlas, it seems to stand alone when compared to other cemeteries on the map. All the others are shown next to churches, and this one is not, perhaps indicating it was a family plot of sorts.

Visitors to the spot will also be struck by the fact that there are no tombstones here, in a plot that is supposed to be a graveyard. Then too, the only reminders to indicate that there might be graves here at all, are shallow pits within the remains of a stone wall that once enclosed the area.

The crumbling stone wall was obviously built to serve as an enclosure, and the faint rows of depressions in the earth within the enclosure seem to provide evidence that these may be gravesites; but neither one of these visual clues proves anything. However, local folktales say that this was once, sadly enough, a cemetery for slaves, and, as hard as it is for us to believe today, the historical record does confirm that the local gentry of that day and age were indeed slaveholders.[5]

John Blair Linn, in his informative *History of Centre and Clinton Counties*, includes numerous references to slaveholders in the valley, including none other than General James Potter who willed "his negro man Hero, and mulatto man Bob" to his son James.[6] It's also interesting to note that General Potter built the first log house and several mills in what is now the little community that was named after him. His descendants inherited those same properties, living and prospering here for many years after the General's death in 1789.

Perhaps the descendants of Hero Wade, the general's old army servant, or others of their race, lived here for many years after General Potter's death as well. If they did, then possibly some of them even once lived in the original store that was built here in 1790 by James Potter, the General's son, and perhaps it is their ghosts that once haunted the present store that sits along the highway there today.

Then again, have the hauntings really ended? Not according to the present store owner, who says that although the ghosts of the Black family seem to be at rest, those of the White family may still be restless. Her feelings on the matter, she notes, are based on an event that happened only several months prior to when she talked to us about her experiences.

"We have a girl who works at the store," explained the storeowner, "and a few months ago she was painting the upstairs apartment for new tenants.

5. Rich Kerstetter, "On Hallowed Ground? Potters Mills May Be Home to a Slave Cemetery," *The Centre Daily Times*, November 24, 2022.

6. Linn, *History*, Ibid, 25.

A Haunted House in Adams County. Located in a secluded setting near Carlisle Springs, this Civil War era dwelling is haunted by the ghost of a Confederate soldier who was shot by the residents of the house in late June, 1863, when they saw him taking a drink from their spring. Local tales say they hung his body in their fireplace until his Confederate comrades departed for Gettysburg. Thereafter, and perhaps yet today, inhabitants of the house heard the sounds of rattling sabers upstairs and felt an invisible entity sit down on the sides of their beds at night. Today they also are occasionally visited by the ghostly image of a young woman wearing a bonnet and faded blue denim dress; supposedly the spirit of a girl who once died of "wasting disease" in the house at some unknown time in the distant past. Just one more example of a haunted homestead nestled along the back roads of the Keystone State.

She said she didn't see it, but she felt the dog! She said her sweatpants were literally being pulled on one side down over her hip, like a dog was pulling them!

"Then another day a guy walked by the doorway of the room she was painting. This happened a few times, but when she looked out into the hall there was nobody! Fortunately, she was good-spirited enough (no pun intended!) that she just said, 'Listen, I've gotta paint for ten more minutes, so just leave me alone for ten minutes, and then you guys can play!' So that was her attitude towards it; so that was good!"[7]

NOTE: When looking at a folktale or legend, it's always fascinating to determine if a similar story appears in the legendary lore of other countries.

---

7. Homan, Ibid.

NO PLACE LIKE HOME

The same can be said for ghost stories too, particularly when it comes to the unusual spectral suicide scene of the Black family at Homan's Store in Potters Mills. Although this tragic portrait may seem unique, it may not be regarded as such if English folklore is explored.

Tales of ghosts bathed in light are not uncommon in England, forming the basis for some of that country's best-known hauntings. There may be many manor houses, castles, and pubs in the British Isles that hold their own "radiant" wraiths, but probably the most well-known one is that of the Radiant Boy of England's Chillingham Castle.

Situated on the border with Scotland in the county of Northumberland, Chillingham, a twelfth-century stronghold used by the English during their border wars with the Scots, is said to hold many ghosts. However, its best-known spirit is that of a young child often sighted in the "Pink Room." Thought to have been "laid," after proper burial was given to a child's skeleton found a number of years ago in the ten-foot-thick wall of the room, the ghost is said to have reemerged in recent years.

Promptly at the stroke of midnight, those near the room say they hear the cries and moans of a young boy, and those who are brave enough to sleep in the room say that as the cries fade away a bright light appears there, and within it appears the blue-clad figure of a boy.[8]

Although the tale of the Radiant Boy is not exactly like that of the "radiant" ghosts in Homan's Store, it does show that there are common traits shared by some tales. What that means is a discussion better left to the experts in such matters, and so that's what we'll do here. Any amateur attempts to scientifically analyze and dissect the events and experiences would only detract from their appeal.

And so, we'll disturb no further the ghosts at the little store in Potters Mills. It can remain, in the words of the poet Longfellow who once wrote of a similar spot, "a place of slumber and of dreams, remote among the wooded hills."[9] Similarly for those who wish to really remember the Potters Mills establishment, there are several other lines in Longfellow's same poem that should help in that regard.

In his "Tales of a Wayside Inn," Longfellow masterfully created impressions about an old-time gathering place that was popular in his day. The

---

8. J. A. Brooks, *Britain's Haunted Heritage*, 186.
9. Emily C. Blackman, *History of Susquehanna County, Pennsylvania*, 183.

words do indeed evoke images of an ancient hostelry that are not far from the scenes one might see if they visit Homan's little shop today.

It too can be described as "somewhat fallen to decay," and it does have the same "weather-stains upon the wall," and "stairways worn, and crazy doors, And creaking and uneven floors" that appear to have been predominant features of Longfellow's quaint spot.[10]

The Wayside Inn, near Sudbury Massachusetts, still stands today where it stood in Longfellow's day, and, like the store in Potters Mills, it is open to the public. But whether or not it ever had its ghosts is not clear from Longfellow's poem. Therefore, Longfellow's description of the Wayside Inn as a "sort of old Hobgoblin hall" may be one that more aptly applies to the store in Potters Mills, especially now that its ghosts have been unmasked.

---

10. Henry W. Longfellow, "Tales of a Wayside Inn," *The Poetical Works of Henry Wadsworth Longfellow*, 232.

CHAPTER 8

PANTHER TRACKS (THEN AND NOW)

"Yep," said the ninety-four-year-old Clinton County farmer, "I've seen panthers three different times, here in the mountains."

We had made a special trip over to Lock Haven to talk with the old gentleman who was born in 1908, and he was proving to be a jovial and delightful link to the past, thereby making the journey worthwhile. Born and raised as a farm boy, our storyteller had grown up in the "Scootac" country of Clinton County. Now he held us spellbound as he was telling us about several panther encounters he had experienced there back in the mid-1920s and mid-1930s while living in the shadows of the Big Tangascootack Mountain.

"The first time, probably about 1925, my brother Joe and I were cutting corn and shocking like the Amish do; you know, the old-fashioned way," explained the old man. "And this panther left out a squall; it was very unusual. We didn't see it, but the squalls kept getting closer and closer and my brother finally said, 'I believe we'll stop cuttin' corn!' (See the chapter titled "Kings of the Hills" in *Volume V* of the author's *Pennsylvania Fireside Tales* series for more details on this encounter).

"The other time I was living on my granddad's farm, which was on the mountains between Monument and Orviston. I was about twenty-eight then and my kids, daughter Joyce, and son Glenn, were about five or six. There was a beautiful house there, but not much else. Three barns had been

A Pennsylvania Panther. "Female, two years old, not full grown."
Taken from W. J. McKnight's Pioneer Outline History of
Northwestern Pennsylvania *published in 1905.*

struck by lightning and burnt down, and there was just a tin shack for a
couple of cows.

"One evening about dusk, the kids come in from the field with the
cows, but they didn't bring the one due to 'freshen' along. So, I took off
and found her about half a mile away in the far corner of one field. She was
in labor; just tremblin' like a leaf! And settin' about thirty feet back in the
woods was this panther! He was waitin' for his evening meal!

"I wasn't comfortable at all, but I went up and petted the cow until
the calf came. Then I threw it over my shoulder and took off, but both the
cow and the panther got up and followed! Once I got back to the farm, I
put the cow and calf in the shack and went in to get my gun. By the time
I got back out, the panther was gone!"[1] To the good fortune of the young
farmer, the formidable predator may have been young and inexperienced.
It had appeared to be more curious than inclined to attack, and it had not
been a large cat.

"Probably only about six feet long from the tip of its nose to the tip of
its tail," was the way the aged mountaineer remembered it from a distance

1. Casper Peters (born 1908), recorded June 21, 2002.

of almost seventy years; and despite a concentrated effort to recall his third panther encounter he finally gave up.

"I can't get it now," he exclaimed. Needless to say, we were disappointed, but the two stories he had told us were enough to remind us just how perilous life could sometimes be when there were still big mountain cats roaming the forests of the Keystone State.

During my earliest story collecting days, I had heard some interesting episodes to prove it, along with some accounts that I collected within the last ten years that indicated that those perilous times may not have ended after all.

The mountain lion was considered more than just a dangerous nuisance by the earliest settlers here in Pennsylvania. These furtive night stalkers caused considerable economic hardships to herdsmen when the felines carried off their livestock, and this was not an uncommon event in the olden time. Often enough it seemed as though you could never be sure where the next "bender" or "painter," two nicknames applied to the wily beasts, was going to show up next. One man who could attest to that fact was old-time mountaineer Seth Nelson of Round Island Station, Clinton County.

Born in 1810, Nelson was 94 when he died at his home in Round Island in 1905. Celebrated as one of the last great hunters of the old stock, his life began during a time when mountain lions and wolves were common sights in the Keystone State. Of course, by the time he died, those animals were mostly a lingering memory in the minds of men who, like himself, once hunted them.

According to his own records, which he kept from 1827 to 1858, he killed "five hundred and thirty three deer, fifty-nine bears, twenty two elks, five wolves, and twelve panthers" during that thirty-two year span.[2] Although he stopped recording his kills after 1858, he continued to hunt well into the last decades of his life, and by some estimates he killed, during that period, the same number of deer, elk, wolves, and panthers as he had killed prior to 1858.

Anyone with that kind of hunting record would have had his share of narrow escapes, and Nelson was no exception. According to the present owners of Nelson's homestead at Round Island, which they now use as a

---

2. Rosa A. Nelson, "Colorful History of a Clinton County Hunter Pioneer of the 1800s," biography of Seth I. Nelson, written sometime in the 1890s and published in the early 1900s, Lock Haven, PA, *Daily Record*. Copy provided to the author by Mrs. R. Caskey of Renovo.

hunting camp, Nelson bought the place from a Captain McClelland in the years immediately following the Civil War, but the house was not exactly in move-in condition. When Nelson arrived there with his family, his children would later recall, there was a panther comfortably ensconced in the second floor of the house.

The large feline had apparently thought it had found a secure den, but Nelson had other ideas. It's not recalled anymore today whether he merely chased the beast away or killed it, but if he did kill it, then it became one of those big cats that could be included in the tallies of panthers killed by Nelson after 1858.[3]

Described as "absolutely fearless" by those who knew him, Nelson never backed down from danger, including the time when he had a "hand to claw" encounter with a female panther. On this particular occasion he was following the trail of a deer he had wounded and was concentrating on trying to find the drops of blood on the path. So intense was his concentration that he almost walked right up to the panther and her two cubs.

Both man and beast immediately reacted defensively, Nelson by raising his gun to fire, and the panther by opening her mouth and hissing at him. Realizing that the panther was about to attack, Nelson pulled the trigger of his gun. However, much to his dismay, the gun didn't fire. It had been raining and his powder had gotten wet, so Nelson resorted to plan B.

He had heard that an attacking panther could be cowed by "looking it right in the eyes," and so he used this tactic to some effect. However, this one continued to advance slowly towards him until it was only three feet away, at which point Nelson reached out with his tomahawk, intending to strike the panther on the head. But, at that point the cat threw up its head so violently that it struck Nelson's hand, causing him to drop the hatchet.

Then, rather than pouncing upon the defenseless man, the panther threw itself on its back and extended its feet in the air, as though awaiting further attack. It gave Nelson just enough time to load his gun with dry powder and shoot the panther in the head. He also killed one of the cubs and captured the other one alive, later selling it before getting back home.[4]

Panthers could prove to be profitable in that era. On one other occasion Mr. Nelson was said to have killed four large panthers on the same

3. Mrs. Robert Caskey, telephone interviews, November 23, 1981 and December 11, 1981.
4. Nelson, Ibid.

Photographic proof? Photo taken in March of 2023 on Big Poe Mountain along the Millheim / Siglerville Pike. The photo is very blurry, perhaps because the photographer's hands were shaking when he took the photo at a somewhat close range! The color version of the photo leaves no doubt that this is indeed a mountain lion.

day, receiving a bounty of twelve dollars for each one. Excellent wages for a day's work during those hard times![5]

Eventually however, the bounty hunting took its toll, and when Nelson died in 1905, most folks thought that the days of the big cats died with him. However, they all might have been surprised to find that there were still a few stragglers that managed to survive, basically because they were probably among the wiliest and stealthiest of the breed.

Herb Cohn and Bert Sellers were two men who might have argued with those who, in 1905, claimed that the panther was a thing of the past in Clinton County. It would have taken a lot of convincing to change either man's mind since it had only been late in the previous year that they both had experienced a panther scare of their own one cool and crisp fall morning in the mountains near Lock Haven.

It happened late in the month of October, when the two men were on their way to work at a cigar factory near Farrandsville. It was barely daylight, and the morning mists still must have been clinging heavily to the hollows and ravines in the mountains, thereby making it difficult to discern objects in the breaking light. The early risers had just passed by W. T. Young's general mercantile and were well out of town when they saw what appeared to be a bear on the road ahead.

---

5. Ibid.

Straining their eyes to see, the young workers finally realized that the animal blocking their way was something else entirely. Then their initial surprise turned to fear when the large animal began to run toward them and finally got close enough for them to see that it was a mountain lion.

Cohn was so frightened that he dropped his dinner pail and took off as fast as he could run, with Sellers not far behind. They had not gone very far when, to their delight, they met K. W. Johnson and Robert Sebring, who, ironically enough, had just started out on a bear hunt. The two were armed with Winchester rifles, and when Cohn and Sellers excitedly told them about the big cat on the road ahead, the men's planned bear hunt turned into a hunt for more exciting big game.

Now, with armed men behind them, Cohn and Sellers turned around and started out running in the direction from which they had just come. When the four men came upon the scene of the panther encounter, they found the beast was still there, calmly feasting upon the contents of Cohn's dinner pail, which had spilled out when he dropped it. A volley of shots soon echoed up the old Carrier Road and down Love Run as Johnson and Sebring fired away.

Later, when describing their kill, the men would recall that the panther "gave one yelp and fell over dead with a bullet through its heart." Johnson had the huge cat mounted and kept it on display at his home for many years afterwards. He took pride in showing his trophy to visitors and in telling them the story of the kill.

His narrative must have been exciting to listen to, and those who heard it were duly impressed when told that the panther measured 12 feet in length. His tale was even more impressive when Johnson claimed that his big cat was "the largest panther killed in this section for years!"[6]

Even though their story was thrilling to hear, Cohn and Seller's panther scare was not nearly as hair-raising as Sam Hinds' encounter the following year. The unusual episode was reported in an article titled "Sam Hinds' Dilemma," which appeared in Thomas Harter's *Keystone Gazette* during August 1905.

"On Tuesday night, Sam Hinds of Mingoville had an experience which will go down as one of the strangest stories in natural history," read the report that appeared in Harter's *Bellefonte Daily* on August 25.

---

6. Author unknown, "A Panther Killed," *Centre Democrat*, October 27, 1904. Article sent to the author by the Bellefonte Historical Society.

Noting that the incident was one "which he will not forget to the longest day he lives," the article went on to describe Hinds' nocturnal brush with death on the night of a "Business Men's Picnic" at nearby Hecla Park. Hinds did not stay at the picnic long.

As foreman of a gang of choppers on a lumber job in Little Sugar Valley, he had promised to be back on the job at the crack of dawn the next day. Besides that, it had started to rain, which had dampened the enthusiasm of the picnickers, and so at eight o'clock, Hinds decided it was time to go. After all, he would first have to return home to change into his work clothes, and then he was faced with a walk of considerable distance through the mountains in the rain to get to the job site.

Even though the darkness and the inclement weather were not conducive to happy thoughts, Hinds was not worried. He knew a short cut and had used it often. It usually took the woods hick an hour and a half, cutting across lots, to get from his house to the job site, and he didn't think it would take much longer tonight. However, he hadn't planned on the unusual delay he was about to experience after making his way through Hecla Gap into Rag Valley, and then over to Little Sugar Valley on nearby Nittany Mountain.

He was making good time, guessing he was about two-thirds of his way there, when he heard a call which he thought was coming from the lumber camp. Glad that he would soon be out of the rain, the bedraggled woodsman hollered back with a shout of delight and then listened intently.

The prompt reply was encouraging, and so the tired man eagerly headed in its direction. He made good progress, until after a quarter of a mile when he recognized his surroundings enough to realize he was heading the wrong way. Now somewhat uncertain as to exactly which way to go from there, he called out once more, but this time his loud hallo was only greeted with silence.

Feelings of fear must have risen in his chest at that point, but Hinds had to have been even more disconcerted when he heard a rustle in the thick brush to his side and then felt something very soft rubbing gently against his shins. At first, he thought it might be a friendly dog, but when he lit a match to get a better look he was surprised. There at his feet he could see "three wooly little creatures," somewhat larger than a common house cat but with bigger heads and long slim tails, playfully scurrying around at his feet.

Still not comprehending what the friendly little beasts might be, Hinds' curiosity rapidly faded when he looked into the dark woods ahead and saw, not twenty feet away, two pairs of glowing eyes staring back at him. A closer look revealed that the fiery eyes were, in both cases, set widely apart, and it made Hinds realize that he was face-to-face with two ferocious panthers—the parents of the little cats at his feet.

His was now a terrible dilemma, and he was struck with sheer terror until he remembered the pack of matches in his shirt pocket. However, when he reached for them, he found that he had forgotten to close the lid of the match box, and at some point when he had bent over, the matches had all spilled out into the soaking rain and onto the wet ground, thereby rendering them useless. Thinking that any movement at all on his part would trigger an attack from the large panthers, Hinds decided to remain as still as possible while the purring cats continued to rub against his legs.

After five minutes of immobility, the frightened man finally decided that enough was enough. Moving would not, he reasoned, put him in any greater peril than just standing where he was. So with a mighty shout, Hinds darted to the nearest tree and placed himself in front of it so that his backside was protected from an attack from the rear. Then within seconds he heard the same rustling noises he had heard before, and soon felt the wooly little animals rubbing up against his legs once again.

Hinds at that point must have realized that he was out of options. He could only stay where he was and hope for the best. At first, he may have felt that his best hopes were coming true when he looked around and saw no signs of either of the little cats' parents, but when he looked at a high ledge of rocks, not twenty feet away and looming high above the horizon, he thought he detected a snake-like movement on its top.

Gradually the shape grew larger and larger until Hinds could see a monster head with golden eyes rise from the ledge. Then the large body of a full-grown panther was soon silhouetted against the night sky.

The cat made no noise as it glowered at him menacingly from its high perch, but the experienced woodsman was struck by the fact that the animal did not have its tail lowered onto the rocks, which would have been a sign of anger. Instead, the beast was holding its tail up in the air and leaning it to the front until it was almost touching its massive skull. It was, Hinds knew from his many years in the woods, a sign of peace, and at that point he resolved to stay right where he was.

All night he stood with his back to the tree, listening to the purring cats at his feet and carefully watching the majestic form on the rocks in front of him. It was not a pleasant spot to be in, and it became even less so when Hinds noted the gleaming eyes of the other big panther staring at him from the woods to his right.

It proved to be a long and nerve-wracking night for the wayfaring woodsman, but about an hour before dawn he was relieved to see the panther on the rocks slide back down and disappear as stealthily as it had first appeared.

Then the purring at his feet ceased as well, and when dawn finally broke all the panthers had melted into the woods like they had been ghosts from an age that many believed had faded away decades ago. As might be expected, to his dying day Hinds would always remember how the call of the panther had led him astray and into danger. It was an experience he cared not to repeat.[7]

Just like those who argued back in 1905 that the panther was a thing of the past, most people today would make the same claims and would contend that there are no longer any mountain lions here in the Keystone State.

On the other hand, there are others who think differently; particularly those acquainted with reliable witnesses who claim to have seen the beasts firsthand in some of the wildest parts of the Pennsylvania mountains within the last five years. One such man is taxidermist Dave Poust of Waterville, Lycoming County, where he conducts his business.

Dave's little shop along the banks of Pine Creek is a magnet for local hunters and devotees of the chase. Drawn here, no doubt, to enjoy genial Dave's hospitality and his well-told hunting tales, visitors to the place will usually also see several fine deer heads with magnificent sets of antlers hanging from the walls of the workshop—products of Dave's polished skills as a taxidermist.

---

7. Author unknown, "Sam Hinds' Dilemma," *Keystone Gazette*, August 25, 1905. Sent to the author by the Bellefonte Historical Society.

Here they also may encounter some other unusual mounted specimens; anything from turkeys to bears, and on some occasions even a mountain lion, albeit of the western variety rather than a local one. On one particular day it was one of those specimens that helped Dave verify that there may indeed still be mountain lions roaming the high peaks of Lycoming and surrounding counties.

"Well, too many people have seen them with the naked eye," claimed Dave one day when we inquired why he believed that there were panthers in that vicinity. "I've had probably ten or twelve people who I know had no reason to lie or exaggerate stop in from time to time to tell me the stories," he went on. He then shared one such account from dependable witnesses whose evidence would have convinced any jury that they were telling the truth. The sighting occurred in 1996, on what Dave referred to as Oak Home Mountain, at the place called Hackett Dead End.

"I had one lady who had a daughter, probably in her thirties, and then I think three granddaughters who were twelve to sixteen years old, and they saw this huge cat-like animal standing in the middle of the road. It was standing broadside, and they got a good look at it. It turned and walked up the road, and they followed it for a ways until it eventually went back into the woods at a place that was mostly open and overgrown with low ferns. But it stood in there for another five minutes, and they got a good look.

"Well, they come in here—we had a flea market going and we were busy. I was at the cash register, and they said 'Oh we just had quite an experience! We just saw a mountain lion!'

"Then they started to tell me where they saw it, and I said—I excused myself, and got the fella that was helpin' me and I said, 'You run the register; I want to talk to these ladies!'

"So I brought 'em over to the shop, and I said 'Now tell me exactly what this lion looked like!'

"Well, they were describing it, and I said 'You all got a good look at it? It wasn't running or just a flash across there?'

"They said, 'Oh no, we watched it ten minutes from the time we first saw it!'

"So I went in here, and I have a mounted bobcat, and I said 'Now there's a mountain lion. This is what you saw.'

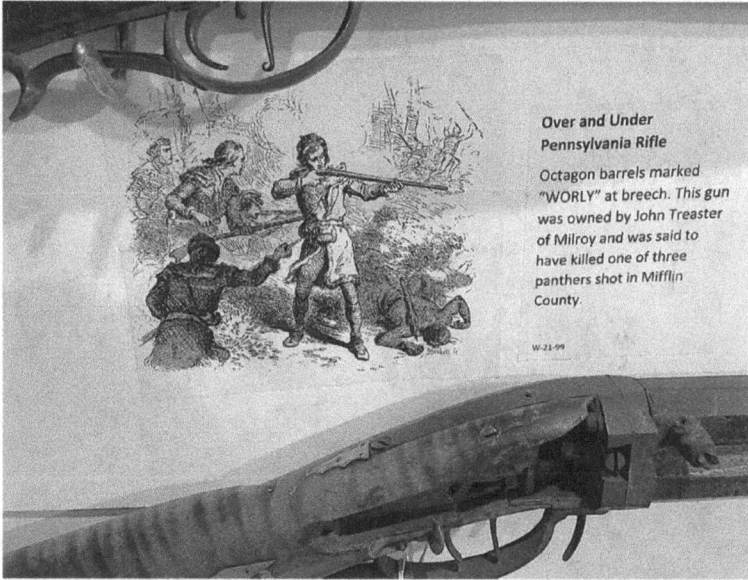

The Last Panther's Nemesis. Inscription describing the rifle used to kill the last panther in Mifflin County—in the display case at the Mifflin County Historical Museum. McCoy House, Lewistown, Pennsylvania. (Photo courtesy of Forest Fisher.)

"And they all looked at each other and said 'Oh no! That's a mountain lion?'

"And I said 'Yeah', and they said, 'Well, then we didn't see a mountain lion!'

"Then I asked them, 'What's different between this and what you saw?'

"And they all agreed that what they saw was 'much larger', with 'a tail close to three feet long' that 'was black on the end!'

"Then I showed them a photo book of mounted specimens we have and asked them to go through it and to let me know if they saw something in there like they saw.

"Well, they were goin' through it and all at once everybody says, 'Yeah, there's what we saw; there it is!' and it was a mountain lion! So I have no question in my mind, because they had no reason to lie."

"Then four years ago during the first day of bear season there were six different hunters with three pairs of long-range glasses looking for bear in the mountains above Jersey Mills. There were six different people there that

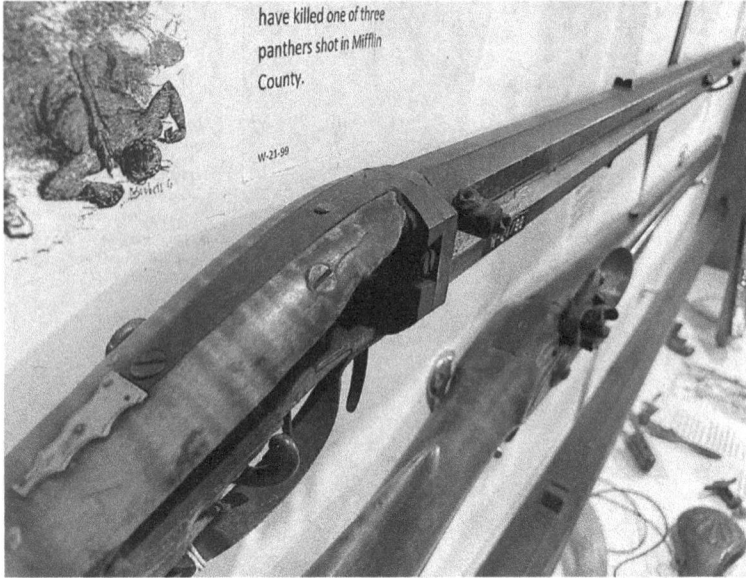

Breech end and long view of The Treaster Rifle. John Treaster used this double-barreled muzzle loader to shoot the last panther in Mifflin County. On display at the Mifflin County Historical Museum in the McCoy House, Lewistown, Pennsylvania. (Photo courtesy of Forest Fisher.)

looked through the three different sets of glasses, and all six verified that they picked up a large mountain lion on the west side of a creek up there.

"Now you can see the eyelashes of a deer at 1200 yards with those glasses. Those guys were not mistaking anything for a mountain lion, but a mountain lion."

In concluding his narrative, the experienced hunter and friend of hunters had this to say about what the Jersey Mills men might have seen that one day when scanning the ridges for bear. "They're all knowledgeable people," emphasized our storyteller, "so if they'd have said they saw a dinosaur, I'd have to believe them!"[8]

There appears to be increasing opinion that the Waterville taxidermist could be right. Even forty years ago the evidence was mounting that *Felis Concolor*, the name that biologists use when referring to the mountain lion, could be making a comeback in Pennsylvania. There were many at that time in some of the western counties who would have sworn that the panther was returning to its old haunts in the mountains. And they would

8. Dave Poust (born 1930) recorded February 27, 1998.

Muzzle end of the Treaster Rifle. Closeup of the muzzle end of the Treaster rifle, showing both muzzles and the octagon shape of the barrels. At the Mifflin County Historical Museum, McCoy House, Lewistown, Pennsylvania. (Photo courtesy of Forest Fisher.)

have based their convictions on a picture that appeared in the Pittsburgh Press about that same time.

The picture left no doubt in anyone's mind. The trophy hanging from the limb of a tree was clearly the carcass of a young panther with a tail that appeared to be almost as long as its body. The photo's caption in fact referred to the beast, which measured five feet three inches from tail tip to nose tip, as a young mountain lion and indicated it had been shot by a local hunter in Venango Township of Crawford County in November of 1967.

Standing on one side of the panther in the photo is the hunter who downed it, and on the other side is a District Game Protector who apparently is inspecting the animal to determine exactly what the state Game Commission's conclusion should be.[9]

To this day the Commission's official stand on the issue of whether or not panthers have returned to the Keystone State is what might be described as adamant. In their opinion all sightings of panthers here in

9. Author unknown, "Mountain Lion Was Killed," photograph with caption, *The Pittsburgh Press*, November 5, 1967.

Pennsylvania are nothing more than cases of "mistaken identity"; tricks of perspective and shadow that cause some to mistake bears, bobcats, foxes, and even ordinary house cats, for bigger game.

In cases like the Crawford County cat, where there is tangible proof that contradicts their official stance, the Game Commission explains it away by offering that the animal was nothing more than someone's pet, which escaped from, or which was released by its owner after he became tired of caring for it once the novelty of having such a companion had worn off.

Despite the hardline posture of the Game Commission, the number of people reporting what to them can be nothing less than a mountain lion has not decreased. This has not seemed to change the Game Commission's stance, however, even though the big cats themselves seem to refuse to accept that they are officially classified as one of Pennsylvania's extinct animals.

NOTE: Among those who would refute the Game Commission's claim that there are no mountain lions here in Pennsylvania might be the following individuals, all who have reason to believe otherwise based on personal and up-close encounters:

A young couple sees a large "feline-like" animal in Halfmoon Valley of Centre County during November of 1999. Describing it as having a large head and long tail, the couple watches the huge beast for some time as it meanders through a farmer's field behind their friends' house.[10]

Around Thanksgiving in 1999, a Ferguson Valley farmer in Mifflin County sees what the thinks is a big dog in one of his fields. However, when he gets out his binoculars for a closer look, he is surprised to see that the "dog" is a mountain lion.[11]

During the October 2005 hunting season, a Clearfield County hunter is "more bewildered than frightened" when a "good-sized cat" passes within 12 yards of the tree he is leaning against to call turkeys. Noting that "there's nothing like it," and that "there's no comparison between a bobcat and a mountain lion," the hunter is sure of what he saw. "I don't know how it got

---

10. Rusty Sodergren, interviewed September, 1999.
11. Susan Stoudt, interviewed December 6, 1999.

there," he is quoted as saying, "but I know what it was!" A year later he is still so absolutely certain that what he saw was a mountain lion that he says he will take a lie detector test to prove it, and even offers to pay for the test if he were to fail![12]

From the windows of her house along the South Mountains of Franklin Township, York County, a woman, in June of 2006, sees an animal that looks "like a circus cat" crouching near her barn, and then watches it move stealthily into a grove of trees growing next to a township building nearby. Describing it as "more streamlined" than a lion or tiger, she sees it well enough and long enough to note its long tail and tawny color. A week later another family in the area reports its horse was attacked, by what appears to be a mountain lion.[13]

Up in Moshannon State Forest along Steel Hollow Road, Centre County, a man coming out of his woodshop around 5:30 AM in September of 2005 sees a pair of bright yellow eyes reflected in his halogen nightlight. Curious as to what kind of animal's eyes would glow that brightly, he turns up the light's intensity and sees a large mountain lion standing by his buck feeder. After running inside to get his wife and daughter, he and his family stand on their back porch and watch the cat for about ten minutes. He estimates the length of the cat's head and body to be five to six feet long and the tail to be three feet long, making the cat's entire length, from nose tip to tail tip, about eight to nine feet. Since then, his neighbors have seen the cat at various times as well.[14]

To bring this narrative up to date, in February of 2024 I received a recent photo of what is no doubt a mountain lion. Taken in March of 2023 along the Millheim-Siglerville Pike on Big Poe Mountain near the Hemlock Acres Campground near the Centre/Mifflin County border, the color photo leaves no doubt as to what the large tawny-colored cat with a long, black-tipped tail might be. The gentleman who took the photo observed the cat for some time before it ambled off into the woods. It seemed to have no interest in attacking him or harming him in any way.[15]

12. Christian Berg, "Mountain Lions Here? Some Swear They Are," *York Daily Record*, January 6, 2006.

13. Author unknown, "Woman Claims She Saw Big Cat," *York Daily Record*, August 5, 2006.

14. Lee Neff (born 1952), interviewed (phone) November 12, 2006.

15. Mitchel Schaeffer, interviewed February 13, 2024.

Perhaps it is sightings like these that have some state officials beginning to question the official government line. In the York County case a wildlife coordinator is quoted as saying that in his Michaux State Forest district there have been, over the years, several other panther sightings which he "deems credible."[16] It would seem, therefore, that if these encounters and sightings continue, it's only a matter of time before no one can dispute the fact that the panther has reemerged as a resident of the Pennsylvania hills it once called home.

HISTORICAL NOTE OF INTEREST:
For decades after the late nineteenth century, there were ongoing accounts of "last panthers" being killed throughout the Commonwealth. For some of those episodes see the chapters titled "The Last Panthers" and "More Last Panther Tales" in the author's *Pennsylvania Fireside Tales Volume VIII*. It seemed fitting, however, to include the following account, not included in *Volume VIII*, in this newly revised and expanded Sunbury Press edition of *Volume VII*, in order to complete the picture of the mountain lion's lifetime in Pennsylvania.

The recollection is an interesting first-hand account of how one of the last mountain lions was shot in Treaster Valley of Mifflin County. The writer signed his article as W. H. G., and so he remains unidentified. Whoever he was, he tended to be fond of long-drawn-out sentences and prone to some grammatical errors in his article, but his descriptions are colorful, and his appreciation of the olden times is evident. I therefore include it here as it originally appeared in the Lewistown Gazette [date unknown, probably 1860s] under the title "One of the Last Hunts for Panthers." As such it provides us with another vivid look into the times when the rugged hunters of nineteenth century Pennsylvania bravely and doggedly pursued and brought to bay some of the biggest game animals which once called our highest peaks their own hunting ground:

"On reading over 'Camping out in the Olden Times' by G. F. in the Gazette several years ago, we readily called to mind a trip made to Treaster Valley in the year 1856 by John Treaster, his son Samuel, Charles P. Ramsey, and his son Will John, and your writer, on a berrying expedition

16. Author unknown, "Woman Claims She Saw Big Cat," *York Daily Record*, August 5, 2006.

sometime in the August month, during which time a ferocious panther roamed at will in this valley. Treaster and son knowing something of the nature of wild animals were armed to the teeth.

Both had good trusty rifles. After a ride of several miles, we alighted from our horses and tied them to trees among the open timber, after which Mr. Treaster, his son, J. W. Ramsey, and your humble contributor, went some distance into the dense undergrowth where the Treasters had a large bear trap set, which on reaching they discovered to be closed, and in it a part of a deer leg, the body being chewed off by the panther, which he no doubt dragged to his abode in the rocks.

The trap was then removed to a large log, over which the animal had dragged the deer, and a hole dug, after which a large pole was brought and one end placed under the log while on the other end, young Treaster, Ramsey, and the writer bore down while John Treaster again set the trap, after which it was lightly covered with leaves. The trail was followed to the creek thru the dense underbrush, where it was followed a short distance, when it crossed the stream and was not followed any farther as it was drawing toward noon.

We then crossed the creek, going perhaps half a mile south, where we found one of the most extensive huckleberry patches that we have ever seen before or since and in less than two hours we had our vessels filled and ready for dinner. The Treasters kept their guns within easy reach all the while, which had a tendency to keep the rest of the crowd on the alert. Each member of the party had two pails, which were placed in grain sacks and carried on the horse, like grandmothers used to do, carry a jug in one end of a bag and a stone of equal weight in the other, but we had berries in both ends.

After filling our vessels we returned to the head waters of that beautiful stream that meanders through that romantic little valley, where we ate our luncheon, after which we again wended our way in a westerly direction toward our respective homes, and we still recollect of one happy fellow in the group when we again came within sight of the Treaster home, as we then imagined that we were not so likely to be torn up by such a ferocious animal.

This same panther was trapped some years later near the place where the trap was set at that time, the animal dragging the trap to the creek, where the grappling became securely fastened among a lot of hemlock roots, from which the water had washed the ground, and Treaster hearing the howling went to the locality and with two or three shots from his unerring rifle he was killed and skinned, the hide being disposed of to Andrew Swartzell, of Milroy, who had it in his possession for many years.

We have forgotten the length of the animal, but think it measured nine feet from the nose to the tip of its tail. This to our recollection was the only panther seen and killed in Treaster Valley during the last 75 years."[17]

COMMENT: It is ironic that a man with the last name of Treaster shot the last panther in Treaster Valley. Likewise, it is also interesting to note that the gun that he used to shoot that last Treaster Valley panther was a double-barreled muzzle loader—a unique weapon in its day; not too common because it was more expensive than single-barreled guns. It is preserved and can still be seen at the Mifflin County Historical Museum in McCoy House, Lewistown. See preceding pages of this chapter for photos of that gun.

17. Old Home Week Committee, *Historical Souvenir of Lewistown, PA*, 52.

CHAPTER 9

GHOST GIRL OF HALFWAY DAM

(And Other Revenants of the "Dark and Bloody Ground")

"Many of our haunted homes are indebted to ancient feuds, in which their owners suffered or inflicted murder," noted John Ingram in his captivating treatise on *The Haunted Homes and Family Traditions of Great Britain*. "And Scotland especially," he continued, "has reaped a crop of ghostly legends and terrifying traditions from the homicidal tendencies of its former notables."[1] Unfortunately, a similar claim might be applied to the Keystone State, but in our case the word notables would be replaced by the words aborigines and colonial settlers.

Chapter three in this volume and chapters in other volumes of the *Pennsylvania Fireside Tales* series include accounts of the homicidal tendencies of both the colonial and the aboriginal populations during the time of Pennsylvania's border wars, and given that fact it should come as no surprise to the reader that the Keystone State, like Scotland, has also reaped its own related harvest of ghost tales and terrifying traditions.

Although the tendency to believe in restless ghosts and mournful spirits created by the conflict between colonials and Native Americans was common to combatants on both sides, those convictions did not disappear after the dust from the last battle between the two factions finally dissipated into thin air. On the contrary, those same ideas, like the ghosts themselves, have stubbornly refused to die and have floated down to us today. And perhaps

---

1. Ingram, Ibid, 286.

The monument at "French" Jacob's mill. Commemorating the four soldiers who were killed here in 1780 by a band of Delaware Indians, it can be found sitting beside Route 192, near the wilds of Raymond B. Winter State Park, Union County.

the reason for that is explained by the fact that the mixed-bag of colonial cultures were just as inclined as the so-called "primitives" to accept that such things were not only plausible, but possible as well.

Probably one of the best examples of how similar the mental processes of early colonists and the Native American tended to be when their thoughts turned to the supernatural realm, can be seen in how they viewed the matter of the unfortunate individuals who met their deaths while tied to an Indian torture stake.

Nothing could have been more horrible than to succumb to the slow and agonizing death that was intended for the captive who was chosen for this fiendish form of entertainment and revenge. A graphic account that shows this to be true, is the description of the tortures inflicted upon Colonel William Crawford. No one died more horribly than him. He was captured while leading a contingent of Western Pennsylvania frontiersmen against Wyandot and Delaware villages along the Sandusky River of the Ohio Country in 1782. Following is that lurid account, and it is not to be read by the squeamish.

After tying their captive to a pole, the warriors, amid wild and fiendish whoops and cries, charged their muskets without ramming any musket balls down the barrel. They then proceeded to take turns discharging their guns at Crawford, their terrible intent being to shoot his body full of hot gunpowder. Then, according to one eyewitness account, "his ears were cut off; burning faggots were pressed against his skin, and he was horribly gashed with knives." This excruciating torture lasted for four hours, ending after the still-conscious man's scalp was torn from his head. He expired shortly thereafter.[2]

As gruesome as their torture of prisoners may have been, and as hard as it is for us today to imagine one human being treating another in this manner, it should be noted that the Native American should not be singled out as being arch fiends in a class way beyond that of European settlers.

Historians who have studied the matter point out that the Indians' monstrous treatment of prisoners may have been something they learned from early Spanish explorers, and that they never exceeded those brutal killers in the cruelty they administered to others. And one final fact should be noted as well, and that is that none of the tortures they devised were more horrific than those that "civilized" Christians inflicted upon one another during the infamous religious persecutions of the medieval period.[3]

Regardless of where the techniques were acquired, the abuses that a victim of Native American tortures had to endure also apparently affected witnesses and torturers alike. According to some historical accounts, those who inflicted the tortures were somewhat frightened by what they had done, after subjecting a prisoner to a long and agonizing death at their torture stakes.

2. C. Hale Sipe, *The Indian Chiefs of Pennsylvania*, 430.
3. Sipe, *The Indian Wars*, 195–196.

One such account, recorded by Sir Edward B. Tylor in one of his interesting cultural studies, notes that following a "riotous night in singeing an unfortunate captive to death with firebrands," North American warriors would howl fiendishly into the darkness and swing branches through the air in order to "drive away the distressed and angry ghost" of their recent victim.[4]

Similarly, colonials also harbored superstitious fears that centered around the sites where torture stakes once stood. One prime example of that is the place the residents of Lycoming and Northumberland Counties once called the Muncy Hills.

Local legends of the West Branch Valley say that sometime during the time the first conflicts between the settlers and aborigines arose here, a party of warriors burned a colonial captive somewhere on the rolling slopes of the hills just south of present-day Muncy, Lycoming County, and about thirty miles north of Northumberland in the county of that same name. Once again, though sad to relate if the local tales can be believed, the poor man's fate was just as hard as that of Colonel Crawford's.

According to this old account, wildly-shrieking warriors "stuck his body full of pitch pine splinters before applying the torch, and danced around him like demons" while they watched him burn to death.[5]

For many years thereafter a barren circular spot on one hilltop marked the place where the immolation occurred. However, despite its longevity, it was remarkable for another reason as well, and that was because no grass or any other living thing, not even the hardier weeds like mullein and burdock, would ever grow there.

It was a circumstance that did not escape notice by superstitious locals, who believed the fallow ground was somehow linked to the hard death experienced by the torture victim. Nonetheless, it was not a unique landmark if similar legends from Adams County can be given any credence.

In a chapter titled "The Lost Brother of Bald Eagle Valley," appearing in the author's first volume of the *Pennsylvania Fireside Tales* series, there is an account of how the Jemison family was attacked by a party of French and Indians in Buchanan Valley of Adams County in 1758.

The historical record is fairly complete when describing the events that befell Thomas Jemison, his wife Jane, and their children, including

4. Edward B. Tylor, *Primitive Culture—Volume 1*, 394.
5. John F. Meginness, *Otzinachson*, 300.

thirteen-year-old Mary, on that particular spring day, and it is fortunate that the accounts were so well preserved.

As it happened, the fate of young Mary was so remarkable and so interesting that the people of Buchanan Valley erected a statue there to commemorate her life. The statue can be seen there yet today (see a photo in my *Volume I*), as can the foundations of the Jemison barn (see the photograph in this volume). But there is also a vestige of that episode that is of a different type, at least according to an old valley legend, and this remnant is as unusual as the life of Mary Jemison.

On the morning that they were captured by four Frenchmen and six Shawnees, the Jemisons were entertaining visitors. William Buck, his sister-in-law, and her three children, had dropped by the previous evening because they had become alarmed over the rumors of war parties in the area and felt there would be safety in numbers. Unfortunately, when the shots rang out it was Buck who was the first to die.

Neighbors later buried Buck not far from where he had fallen, marking the grave with a mound of field stones. For years afterwards the spot was also easily identified by two large maple trees that stood at the edge of a nearby narrow ravine. There was also another close landmark that once led seekers to this spot, in the form of an old apple orchard, whose gnarled and twisted survivors formerly served as a source of fresh fruit for the Jemisons.

No doubt apples from those same trees once provided fresh "squeezin's" for apple cider too, but those pleasant times were soon forgotten after the unsettling events of that spring day in 1755. As orchardists will attest, an apple orchard's productivity declines over time as the apple trees get older, and this one was no different.

Eventually the trees no longer bore any fruit, and local farmers began to cut them down and plow up the orchard to break ground for a new field. Soon thereafter, however, those who plowed among the old trees noticed that there was one spot where the soil was blood red rather than dark brown like the surrounding earth.

It took some discussion and enquiries into local history, but those who looked into the matter finally agreed that the vermillion-colored spot must have been the exact place where William Buck was shot by the war party on the day the Jemisons were captured. It was his blood, so the superstitious farmers agreed, that had soaked into the soil here, permanently staining it

Remains of the Jemison homestead on the Glatfelter Paper Co. lands. Picture taken in Adams County by the author during a pleasant outing with librarians of the York County Libraries during May, 2006. It was experiencing history firsthand to actually walk on the path Mary Jemison once trod and to touch stones that she may also have once touched.

with the crimson tones that would forever mark the place where Buck met his tragic end.[6]

Strange spots on the ground are one thing, but when it comes to supernatural links to Pennsylvania's border wars, many people wonder about the ghosts those wars may have produced. Not surprisingly, there have certainly been a few of those kinds of revenants, along with some individuals who claim to have seen them.

Over in the Muncy Hills, for example, it was once widely believed that, on certain nights of the year when the night winds wailed in the gloomiest glens and caused weird and fanciful shadows to dance on the hillsides, the ghosts of those slain in a battle between settlers and Indians, that occurred in September of 1763, could be seen and heard here as well.

The historical record has little to say about that battle, but local sources indicate that a company of about one hundred volunteers from the counties

6. Ibid, 40–51.

More foundations of the Jemison homestead on the Glatfelter Paper Co. lands, viewed by the author and York County Librarians.

of Lancaster and Cumberland battled a large war party at this spot, hoping "to punish them for the numerous murders and depredations committed by them on the frontier settlements of those counties."[7]

It is said that on the first night of the battle the combatants were so close that each side could hear the other cocking their guns and could also hear the moans and groans of the dying and wounded. It was the ghosts of the combatants that died here that some individuals later claimed to see, and it was their ghostly groans they claimed to hear when passing over these same hills at night.

There were, of course, those who claimed that anyone seeing or hearing ghosts on the Muncy Hills was merely imagining things, and that certainly could be true in some cases. As a matter of fact, it would probably be true in enough cases that the doubters would also feel justified in making similar accusations about others who have encountered Pennsylvania's ghosts of the "dark and bloody ground."

---

7. Ibid, 295–300.

Another view of other Jemison homestead foundations that, in 2006, could still to be seen on the Glatfelter Paper Co. lands.

On the other hand, many of those who experienced these ghostly visitations first-hand would not be so likely to concede that their imaginations were playing tricks upon them. However, in the end, of course, it all boils down to personal opinions and beliefs. Therefore, in order to help readers decide for themselves, I think the following accounts may be of interest.

The description of Pennsylvania as the "dark and bloody ground" is one that has been used to refer to the Keystone State when talking about its times of border warfare. As one historian has noted, "The period of Border Wars in Pennsylvania is one of the most thrilling and bloody chapters in American history. Pennsylvania suffered more than did any other of the Colonies during this long period stretching from 1755 to 1795."[8]

Other accounts in the *Pennsylvania Fireside Tales* series also make it clear that the preceding description is not an inappropriate one, and anyone who has read the historical records of that era will readily concur.

There are undoubtedly many ghostly annals confirming this horrific description too, and one of the legends typical of those archives is based

8. George P. Donehoo, in C. Hale Sipe's *The Indian Chiefs of Pennsylvania*, introduction.

on the remains of an old stone foundation and water well which are visible yet today not far from the well-preserved home of Conrad Weiser, Indian agent for the Penn family, near Womelsdorf in the Tulpehocken Valley of Berks County.

Located along Charming Forge Road, which leads to the pleasant little community of Charming Forge, the remains of the old well and a nearby home site are hardly noticeable anymore. The two-foot-high stone foundation is now thickly overgrown with weeds and is shaded by a large copse of trees, but if you stop and take a closer look you will also see the tops of the stone walls which once shored up the well that was the source of water for the family that settled there.

The well seems to have been filled up with stones sometime in the past, and so it no longer serves as a source of water for anyone, but it is this well which is the source of the ghostly legend that clings to this same spot.

According to the local legend that was once familiar to students who attended Conrad Weiser High School, there was a family of German settlers living in a cabin beside the well sometime in the 1750s. One fall day, when the men were away hunting, a party of warriors crept up to the cabin and shot and scalped the young woman who was there with her twin babies.

However, the old account also relates that the raiding party was not satisfied with the one victim they had already claimed, and so took the twin babies and dashed their brains out on the rock walls of the well. Years later there were people who, when passing by the well on Halloween night during the time of an Indian Summer, said they could hear the cries of those innocent babes, sounding just like they must have sounded when they were torn from the arms of their mother.

Even down to the present day there are people who say the same sounds can still be heard there on Halloween. More skeptical folks say it's just the night wind soughing in the tops of the trees that now grow at this place. Despite whatever the source of the sound may be, there are few today who stop by to listen.

As a consequence, perhaps those sounds, if they were the wails of the spirits of babies whose lives were snuffed out almost as soon as they began, have ceased because there is no one left who comes to comfort them.[9]

Indifference or lack of caring, on the other hand, may be what keeps another victim of the scalping knife from finding eternal rest. The main

9. Sean Young, interviewed September 13, 1996.

reason no one may pay much attention to this restless spirit, if she does indeed exist, may be because she seems to be a shy ghost or a frightened one.

And for that reason, her vapory form may find it hard to attract the energy it needs to materialize very often. However, every once in a while, the ghost girl of Halfway Dam does garner enough energy to appear to travelers who are driving through Raymond B. Winter State Park, the name now assigned to this natural beauty spot.

There were many who were probably opposed to the name change, when Halfway Dam State Park became Raymond B. Winter State Park in 1957. Although the new name was to honor long-time District Forester Ray Winter, who devoted a large part of his life to the upkeep and protection of this place, traditionalists preferred the original name.

Their nostalgic preference for the original title was its historic underpinnings and the history it recalled. It was a romantic retrogression to an old roadside inn called the Halfway House that stood here when the park grounds were purchased by the state in 1905.

The inn itself derived its name from the fact that it sat midway along the 14-mile-long Brush Valley Narrows, a route traversed by PA Route 192 today, which connects the towns of Livonia, Centre County, and Forest Hill, Union County. Back in that time there was also a nearby sawmill dam that could be seen here too, before it was replaced by another, and that dam was the other landmark from which the park got its original name.

Constructed to replace the much-deteriorated sawmill dam, the new one built here in 1933 by crews of the Civilian Conservation Corps, most often referred to in those days as the CCC, was the first stone masonry dam built by the CCC in the United States. Still standing today and fed by the waters of Rapid Run and Halfway Run, the stone wall of the dam forms a six-acre lake which provides a nice swimmin' hole for locals in the summer months and fine trout fishing for anglers in fishing season.

The 400 acres of park land, and many more acres of surrounding Bald Eagle State Forest land, also attract hikers who like to enjoy the cool heights of nearby Naked Mountain, Sand Mountain, and Seven Notch Ridge. But with so many "miles to wander," there are many potential hiding spots here as well, and hiding somewhere in the dark hollows and other mystic places of the dense forest along Route 192 may be the last faint particles of the park's ghost.

At least one young woman thinks so. The young lady had just completed her 3:00 P.M. to 11:00 P.M. shift at Lewisburg Evangelical Hospital one July night in 2005, and was heading back along Route 192 to her home in Rebersburg, Centre County. It had been one of those July dog days, and the oppressive heat and humidity had turned into a downpour at 6:30. The deluge lasted until about 9:30 that night, but much of the earlier rain had turned to heavy fog when it met the hot asphalt paving of the highway.

The dense fog forced the tired hospital worker to creep along Route 192 at a snail's pace even though she was the only car on the road at this late hour. The slow speed was not unwelcome, she realized, since it afforded her a chance to indulge in a more pleasant activity. Consequently, she took the opportunity to roll down her car windows so she could enjoy the smell of the summer rain and the fresh scents of the rain-soaked forest.

In the ghost girl's woods, where she was seen by the nurse that hot July evening. R. B. Winter State Park, Union County.

She had always liked the fragrances of campfire woodsmoke and any other odors that reminded her of the woods, and tonight was just another opportunity to enjoy some of them. Although the dense fog caused her to drive more slowly than usual, the late-night traveler was also worried about deer crossing the road at this hour too, and when that thought came to mind, she slowed down even more. By this time, it had taken her about twenty minutes to reach Raymond B. Winter Park after passing through Forest Hill, and it was then that she reached a sharp turn in the road.

She decelerated to navigate the curve, but after coming through it she was surprised to find that the road ahead was clear for some distance before the fog blanketed it again. Then she was even more surprised as her car came out of the curve and her headlight beams illuminated the right side of the highway.

At first, she thought it was just a patch of white fog that had drifted out of the deep woods on the left or had rolled onto the road from off the steep mountain on the right. Then when she looked more closely, she realized that the "cloud" now appeared to be the figure of an eight- or nine-year-old girl who was running at top speed in order to cross the highway.

Caught completely off guard by the sight, the driver's initial reaction was to wonder what a little girl of that age was doing out by herself at this late hour and on a bleak night like this. Then, to her horror, the bemused woman suddenly realized that although she could see some of the figure's distinguishing characteristics quite clearly, she could also see right through it, almost like looking through a slightly translucent pane of glass.

Although her glimpse into the unknown lasted less than a minute, it was distinct enough for the shaken onlooker to know that the colorless impression was that of a barefooted girl wearing pig tails and an old-fashioned dress with puffy sleeves. The other thing that also seemed apparent was that this image of the air never looked back at the young woman who was staring at it in disbelief.

The image seemed to convey the idea that it was frightened by something and only interested in getting away from its observer, or from unseen attackers, as quickly as possible, almost as though she were running for her life.

At that point, as far as the driver of the car was concerned, she wanted to get away as quickly as possible too. It had finally dawned on her that she had just seen a ghost, and she didn't want to hang around to see what might happen next. Later, however, she learned from coworkers that the old-time spirit of Halfway Dam, when in human form, may have had good reason to run for her life, given the many tales of Indian massacres in this same section.[10]

Based on those accounts, could it be that this ethereal little woods-nymph, when in human form, was a victim of a war party that massacred a family near here? Although attempts today to discover the identity of the terrified little spirit, and the sad story which led it to its fate, would most likely be fruitless, there just may be clues buried in the region's historical record.

The clues, if you can call them that, are only faint ones, but they do offer one possible explanation behind the apparent terror that is exhibited by the ghost girl of Halfway Dam, assuming you are lucky enough to see her, or are willing to concede that such things are possible. Those faint suggestions appear in the documented colonial history of the region. They do without doubt substantiate that Union County and neighboring Snyder County felt the brunt of Pennsylvania's border warfare, beginning with the French and Indian War and extending through the Revolutionary War.

Those terrible times began with the very first intrusion of embold-ened war parties into Pennsylvania, following General Braddock's defeat by French and tribal allies in western Pennsylvania during the summer of 1755. Those incursions in October of that same year resulted in a two-day period when settlers along Penn's Creek, Snyder County, and from New Berlin in Union County to Selinsgrove in Snyder County were massacred almost non-stop. However, that was only a taste of what was to come.

Numerous Union County incidents could be mentioned as well, like the murder of Major John Lee's family near Winfield, Union County, in 1782, described as "one of the most revolting crimes of the Pennsylvania frontier."[11] On the other hand, there seem to be no similar historically-con-firmed incidents that occurred near present-day Raymond B. Winter State Park other than an attack on a patrol of Continentals near "French Jacob's" mill in the spring of 1780.

Jacob Grozean's old wooden mill bore the evidence of his battles with scalp-hunting warriors as long as it stood near the small spring which fed it.

10. Desiree Leitch, telephone interview, July 16, 2006.
11. Sipe, *The Indian Wars*, 675.

The "Frenchman's Spring," as locals often called it, derived its name from the fact that it was here that Grozean (or Groshong, as some historians spell it) once successfully hid himself from marauding warriors who were pursuing him.[12]

The little spring still bubbles up at this same spot today, but the old wooden mill with the bullet holes in its siding disappeared long ago. However, there is one reminder of that mill that still stands along Route 192 at the present time, and it commemorates the murder of the Continentals that occurred here over 220 years ago.

About seven miles east of Raymond B. Winter Park, and only about one-half mile from the old Forest House Hotel, there is a vertical stone monument standing on the north side of the highway at the intersection of Buffalo (Route 192) and Wabash Roads. Today most motorists whiz by the old marker, not stopping to read the inscription on the metal plaque attached to the stone, and one reason for that is the busy lifestyle of the present age.

Then, too, the monument is easily missed because of the way it blends in with its surroundings. However, those who notice the unusual monolith, and take the time to pull over and read its epitaph, will learn about a fragment of almost-forgotten Buffalo Valley history.

On the monument's metal plate are the names of four men who, along with their fellow comrades, were literally "caught with their pants down" one spring day in 1780, when they had just returned from a patrol. They were there to protect the mill and the surrounding settlers, but after their sweep of the area the men decided to let down their guard and take a refreshing dip in the creek.

As the soldiers cooled off in the invigorating waters, they were attacked by a party of stealthy warriors who had somehow avoided detection when the young Continentals were on patrol. Four of the men were killed in the attack, and at least one of them lost his scalp. It is that incident that the Union County Historical Society wanted people to remember when they erected the marker in 1922.

Yet as interesting as the old monument may be, it brings us no closer to identifying a possible candidate for the young lady whose ghost now haunts the area once known as Halfway Dam. The best we can do, it would

12. John Blair Linn, *Annals*, 182.

seem, is to provide the reader with one more anecdote that shows how a family of settlers in Dry Valley of Union County reacted to a party of raiding warriors intent upon taking their scalps during the time of the Great Runaway in 1778.

Linn, in his entertaining *Annals of Buffalo Valley*, recalls an incident that was passed down to later generations by "old Mrs. Fought," who experienced the horrible events first-hand. On what was developing as a normal working day in 1778, the Foughts were busy threshing flax at their homestead in Chappel's Hollow when a party of warriors swooped down upon them without any warning.

There was only enough time, Mrs. Fought would later lament, to pick up her baby and run for her life. Unfortunately, however, it meant she had to abandon her other child, a mere toddler who was playing in back of their barn, since the enemy warriors were closing in too fast. Alarmed as well, the toddler saw its mother running away and called after her in plaintive tones.

The brave woman escaped, but until the day she died she was haunted by the memory of the child she left behind, never giving up hope that she would somehow find it and bring it home. She was tormented the rest of her remaining years, not only at nighttime but even in "the quiet hours of the day," by her child's last words, "O mother, take me along too!"[13]

It's not a satisfying or happy ending to our little chapter, but no ghost story ever satisfies the curious seeker who is looking for proof that life goes on in the next world. There never is a conclusive ending to such tales because all clues embedded in them are faint ones. And so it is that we must leave our little Halfway Dam ghost to her wanderings. Perhaps she will find peace one day, if she hasn't already, but if she is not yet at rest then maybe she will reappear from time to time to those who wish to solve her mystery and hope to penetrate the boundaries of the world to come.

---

13. Ibid, 159.

CHAPTER 10

QUEEN ESTHER'S ROCK

Although a number of ghost and supernatural tales arising from Pennsylvania's period of Native American warfare were recorded in the last chapter, there are two other tales similar to those that deserve a chapter of their own. Another reason for the segregation is that repercussions of the events that serve as the basis for the tales have been mentioned several times in this volume, and in others of the *Pennsylvania Fireside Tales* series.

It therefore seems appropriate to start with some mention of the 1778 events that occurred in the Wyoming Valley of Luzerne County, which emboldened Native American warriors to attack other settlements along the Pennsylvania frontier during that same year. These bloody attacks created a widespread panic all across the frontier and caused most settlers to abandon their farms and homesteads; an evacuation later described by historians as the Great Runaway.

Although the historical record is clear on most aspects of the Wyoming Valley events, the legendary record has something to say about the matter as well, and it is that record that we want to explore in this chapter to see if it contains any facts that may have escaped the watchful eye of the historian. Consequently, we'll end the chapter with the two tales mentioned in the first paragraph: one being a ghost episode whose origins might be traced back to the events that took place in the vale of Wyoming in 1778, and the other, which adds a supernatural twist to the lurid story of Queen Esther's Rock.

Of all the outrages and massacres that occurred in the Wyoming Valley between the years 1763 and 1781, the one that is most remembered is the massacre of Colonel Zebulon Butler's forces on July 3, 1778. On the day before, July 2nd, a force of 400 British soldiers and Tories (Americans who were British sympathizers), along with 700 Seneca warriors, attacked and captured Forts Wintermoot and Jenkins, at or near present-day West Pittston.

Several other small forts, all within limits of present-day Wilkes-Barre, capitulated on the same day, because of the lack of cannons inside the forts and the lack of able-bodied defenders (most of the valley's men were off fighting with the Continental Army). However, the events of July 2 were merely a preview of the horrible defeat that was to follow the next day.

Colonel Zebulon Butler, on leave from his duties in the Continental army and aware of the events of the previous day, took charge of the settlers who were left on July 3. The forces he had left to protect them hardly seemed adequate; since his recruits, mostly old men and young boys, were unseasoned and untrained troops. And without doubt an objective observer would not have given them a ghost of a chance of defeating the enemy that was on their very doorstep.

Nonetheless, on July 3, Colonel Butler rallied his forces at the stockade whose name was derived from the first settlers who built it. They were Connecticut men, and there were forty of them. So, it was at Forty Fort that Butler took his stand.

The seasoned Colonial thought he could hold the old bastion until reinforcements arrived, but more petulant personalities prevailed, including that of hot-headed Lazarus Stewart, leader of the infamous Paxton Boys who had murdered innocent Conestogas sheltered in the Lancaster County jail in 1763.

Caving in to the urgings of his troops, Colonel Butler allowed them to leave the fort to attack the enemy, but before letting them go on their sortie he reminded them of the danger they were facing.

"Men," said Butler in grave tones, "yonder is the enemy. The fate of the Hardings tells us what we have to expect if defeated!"[1]

The reference to the Hardings was an appropriate one. Not only because of its effect of impressing upon the men the danger they were about to face, but also because it touches upon the legendary realm of the story, which

---

1. Sipe, *The Indian Wars*, 550.

Penn's Treaty with the Indians under the Shackamaxon Oak in 1683. Commissioned by Thomas Penn and painted by Benjamin West, it depicts the legendary treaty agreed to by Penn and Lenni Lenape chief Tamanend. Photo taken by the author at the Conrad Weiser Homestead historical site in Womelsdorf, Berks County.

we will explore in more detail later. Suffice it to say for now that Butler's warning was ignored by the outnumbered patriots, and of the 400 who left the fort to do battle, only 60 survived.

The others, including the impetuous Stewart, were either shot down like dogs during the fight, or cruelly tortured to death once captured. Unfortunately, so many local militiamen were slaughtered and the valley left in such a sorrowful state that those forts that remained were said to be "filled with widows and orphans."[2]

As details of the terrible massacre reached settlers along the north and west branches of the Susquehanna, a general panic quickly became widespread, and many took flight. Soon, except for the towns of Sunbury and Northumberland, there were no northern outposts left to stand against the rising tide of Tories and Indians, and even in those two places only the bravest of the brave stayed behind. It appears everyone else was thoroughly intimidated by the emboldened warriors, who now swept down upon larger groups of settlers than they were ever bold enough to attack in the past.

---

2. Day, Ibid, 439.

And if that reality, and the news of the fall of Forty Fort, were not enough to turn even the bravest men into more cautious ones, the mere details of what happened at Forty Fort and the fate of the Wyoming Valley survivors after the Forty Fort defeat would have been the turning point for many.

Names of the Seneca chiefs who led the attack against Forty Fort were no doubt included in the accounts of the battle that reached the frontier. The chiefs' names would have been familiar to many, not only because these warriors had such fierce reputations as hardened foes of the European encroachers but also because they were known for their ferocity when in battle. And so it was that the names of Red Jacket, Big Tree (*Ga-Oun-Do-Wah-Nah*) and "He-who-goes-in-the-smoke" (*Gi-En-Gwah-Toh*) became intertwined with the history of the valley.[3]

Accounts of that terrible time in Luzerne County form a historical record that for us today lends credence to the old adage that truth is stranger than fiction. On the other hand, it's also been said that the annals of the Wyoming Valley's original families "form a romance of themselves." What that in turn means, in the opinion of one prominent historian, is that "folklore has been hard at work on the Battle of Wyoming," producing "a number of distortions that need to be corrected."[4]

Exaggerations and distortions about the battle were no doubt included in the graphic details of the battle's outcome that eventually created a high level of consternation and fear along the upper stretches of the Susquehanna. Undoubtedly included in those lurid accounts would have been seemingly unbelievable but totally accurate descriptions of the aftermath. They would tell of how, that night, the blaze of burning buildings lit up the entire valley. They would also describe terrified survivors, some who had been scalped alive, fleeing to the relative safety of the Pocono Mountains beyond Stroudsburg to the north.

In addition, the graphic narrations about the confusion, devastation, and bloodshed would have also undoubtedly included an account of all the people who had survived the brandished tomahawk and scalping knife only to meet death in the terrible wilderness they had to pass through on their way to what they thought would be a place of refuge. And these were

3. Sipe, *The Indian Wars*, 556; and Day, Ibid, 438.
4. Paul A. W. Wallace, *Indians in Pennsylvania*, 161–62.

the spots, these wilderness dying places, where the most fatalities occurred due to exposure, starvation, and the like, that were later referred to as the "Shades of Death."[5]

As terrible and frightening as the descriptions of the attack on Forty Fort and the narrations about the Shades of Death might have been, they probably paled in comparison to the scenes of horror that were brought to mind when people heard about the events that occurred after the battle at another place in the valley; a place that would become known to history as "Queen Esther's Rock."

And it was no doubt the accounts of the activities that took place here that left many settlers along the West Branch "doubtful," in the words of militia Colonel Samuel Hunter, "whether tomorrow's sun shall rise on them freemen, captives, or in eternity."[6]

There is some doubt, however, that surrounds the accounts of what took place at that infamous rocky outcrop still pointed out today as "Queen Esther's Rock," and it is perhaps at this boulder where folklore has been hardest at work and has created a number of apparent distortions.

Historians disagree about who actually committed the atrocities that took place at the infamous rock. Although there seems to be consensus that a woman was the bloodthirsty fiend who performed the dastardly acts, there is some confusion about who she was and what whipped her into a killing frenzy; and that's where history ends, and valley legends pick up the thread.

Historical accounts agree that the gallant defenders of Forty Fort were "slaughtered without mercy" and that those who lived to surrender were "subjected to the most cruel torture."[7] Those same accounts also agree that the cruelest and most gruesome episode of the many that occurred that fateful day, was when sixteen of the staunchest captives were arranged in a circle around a large rock, which is there yet today, rising to a height of about eighteen inches off the ground.

After the men were forced to kneel and place their heads upon the boulder, a hysterical woman, identified by some as the Munsee woman known to the captives as Esther Montour, began to dance wildly around the stone. The frenzied performance was probably remarkable for a number of

---

5. Sipe, *The Indian Chiefs*, 488–89.
6. Carl Carmer, *The Susquehanna*, 135.
7. Sipe, *The Indian Wars*, 550.

*Queen Esther's Rock. The Bloody Rock as it looks today with its protective
cover. Along Susquehanna Avenue in the city of Wyoming, Luzerne County.*

reasons, including the dancer's unearthly screams and the large tomahawk
she waved around in the air over her head.

However, the ghastliest memory left on the minds of those who saw
the "dance" was the part where the woman, undoubtedly with a look of
fury and hatred frozen upon her face, stopped now and then, as though
she were playing some macabre game of Russian Roulette, to dash out the
brains of a captive kneeling before her.

Although tradition has perpetrated the idea that the "priestess" who committed the many murders at the rock was Esther Montour, historians do differ on the matter. There are those, on the one hand, that point out the kinder nature of Esther's mother and grandmother, and conclude that Esther's inherited personality traits would be that of a gentle woman, rather than the she-devil who became known as the "fiend of Wyoming." On the other hand, different historians indicate that Esther may not have even been in the Wyoming Valley at the time at all, and also point out how, at the start of the Revolutionary War, she treated the Strope family, her prisoners at the time, "with great kindness."[8]

However, George Peck in his 1858 history of Wyoming County believed otherwise, stating "we see no good reason for doubting the part attributed to Catherine Montour, or Queen Esther, in the affair of the Bloody Rock."[9] On the other hand, it can be noted that Peck may have confused Esther Montour with her sister, "French" Catherine Montour, who also had reason to harbor an intense hatred of colonial settlers.

After all, it was Catherine's town along Seneca Lake, in present-day Schuyler County of New York State, that was singled out by General John Sullivan as the first town to be destroyed on his punitive expedition into the Iroquois lake country; but that occurred a year later—in the summer of 1779. Therefore, Peck offers a reason why it was most likely Queen Esther who became a killing machine that day around the Bloody Rock.

"It was a right," notes Peck, "if not, indeed, the duty of the old queen to take sweet vengeance upon the prisoners which had fallen into her hands for the loss of her son who had been killed by a scouting party before the battle."[10]

Peck offers no further details about the death of Esther's son or the names of the scouts who may have killed him, but this is the place where valley legends pick up the story and offer some explanations of their own.

"One of the Hardings and his brother were partly responsible for the Wyoming Massacre," claimed one of Pittston's native sons one day when he was telling us about the folktales and legends of the area.

"During the time of the Indian wars, war parties were coming down along the Susquehanna River, and all the people went down and gathered

8. Wallace, Ibid, 172.
9. George Peck, *Wyoming: Its History, Stirring Incidents, and Romantic Adventures*, 290.
10. Ibid, 285.

in Forty Fort and waited for them," continued the man who had heard the old tales of colonial warfare while growing up in the area.

"Well, time went by, and they didn't show up, and so the Harding brothers figured 'the hell with this', and they went back upriver to work their fields, since they had crops they needed to tend to. Then while they were working in their fields, two warriors appeared on the scene and fired at the harvesters. The shots killed one of the Hardings, but the other Harding fired at the Indians and killed one of them, who was just a young boy. Well, it turned out that this young boy was Queen Esther's son!

"That's why she went crazy after they took everyone prisoner at Forty Fort. She lined up all the settlers and she painted herself all up black and white, and one at a time she mashed their heads against the rock. Some broke and started running in all different directions, and a few made it to the river, escaped by swimming across, and told the story. I heard that as a kid!"[11]

Although the historical annals of the valley aren't quite that specific, they do note that, on the 30th of June, Benjamin, Stuckley, and "young John" Harding, along with six other men, "went up the river from Wyoming into Exter to labor in their fields." Perhaps lulled into a false sense of security by the calm and balmy days of June, the men worked all morning and all afternoon without incident, but late in the afternoon they were attacked by a war party who killed five of the nine, including two of the Hardings.

Three others were taken prisoner, but young John Harding managed to escape by diving into the Susquehanna, at a place where several large willow trees were growing along the bank with their lithe branches hanging down over the water. The resourceful pioneer lad, hoping to avoid detection, concealed himself among the willow boughs while just keeping his mouth above water in order to breathe.

The warriors made a long and careful search for the escapee, and "at one time," Harding would later relate, "they were so close to me that they could have touched me." After his long submersion, the young pioneer did manage to escape, make his way back to the relative safety of the settlements, and tell them of the terrible fate of his brothers and the other men who had forfeited their lives in order to tend to their crops.[12]

---

11. Ken Davis (born 1937), interviewed March 2, 1972.
12. Sipe, *The Indian Wars*, 549.

The following day, after John Harding had told them of the massacre, a small detachment of militiamen marched the eleven miles from Forty Fort to Exter in order to bury their fallen comrades. The appearance of the dead men must have been an unsettling sight, even to the hardened frontiersmen, for the dead bodies indicated that each man had given his last full measure before being killed.

All of the bodies had been scalped and mangled, but the faces and arms of Benjamin and Stuckley Harding had been "frightfully cut" and there were "several spear holes" through their torsos, indicating either the intensity with which they had fought for their lives, or which were inflicted on their dead bodies by warriors that may have held a special grudge against them.[13]

These same historical accounts don't indicate whether the Hardings or any of their fellow victims killed any of those warriors during their struggle on the fields of Exter, on what may have been an otherwise pleasant June afternoon in 1778. Therefore, it can't be said with any certainty that the Hardings killed Queen Esther's son that day.

However, on the following day before the burial party began their gruesome task, two warriors who had concealed themselves in the woods besides the field and hoped to ambush any colonials who came to take the bodies away were, themselves, ambushed and killed by the burial detail.[14]

In an odd twist of fate, if local legendary accounts are to be trusted, one of those killed turned out to be Gencho, the only son of Queen Esther. The men in the burial detail had no way of knowing who the two warriors they had killed might be, and so, in their rage and fury, the frontiersmen who shot Gencho made matters worse by also scalping him and mutilating his body with their tomahawks and knives.

It was this act of desecration, locals still believe, that most likely turned Queen Esther into the bloodthirsty fiend who dashed out the brains of thirteen helpless frontiersmen three days later, around what was to become known to history as the "bloody rock."[15]

The Wyoming massacre was the last straw for General George Washington. He had finally had it with the harassments of the Six Nations; and so, exactly one year later, following continuing massacres, he ordered

13. Ibid.
14. Ibid.
15. Ken Davis, Ibid.

General John Sullivan to take five thousand seasoned troops into the heart of the Iroquois country and break the power of the great confederacy by destroying their villages.

In the summer of 1779, the "town destroyer," as the Iroquois would later call him, and his troops, marching out appropriately enough from Fort Wyoming, departed on their mission of devastation. It was a task that was completed with a thoroughness that was only to be seen again in wars of the modern era. At the end of their spectacular mission, Sullivan's army and its detachments, including General James Clinton's forces, destroyed almost fifty Indian towns in the Genesee Valley of New York State. It was considered a spectacular success, since despite the risks and dangers, "only forty soldiers were lost by sickness and to the enemy."[16]

It's unfortunate that the names of all forty casualties of Sullivan's expedition, as well as those who fell at Forty Fort, were not preserved for posterity; and it is perhaps for that reason that at least one of those forgotten men could not, and perhaps still cannot, find eternal peace. Or at least that might be one explanation for the origins of a frightening specter that once haunted an old boarding house that stood about five miles west of where Fort Wyoming once served as a protective bastion to the settlers of the Wyoming Valley.

Fort Wyoming was located "on the river common" and "about eight rods southwest of the junction of Northampton and River streets in the city of Wilkes-Barre" according to the panel of historians who were charged with investigating the matter.[17]

Near this historic spot once stood an old boarding house, a primitive log cabin which was one of the first ones built in the town of Nanticoke. Given its early origins, it is not surprising that it was regarded as a haunted place, and for good reason. Its ghost seemed to prefer the same room in the old place, and it may have haunted the establishment from the time it was built.

It did not always make its presence known, but when it did choose to shape itself into a recognizable form in the wee hours of a morning, it scared the wits out of anyone occupying the room. This in turn also created stress for the landlady when occupants would hastily leave the next

---

16. Sipe, Ibid, 604, 741.
17. Thomas L. Montgomery, ed., *Frontier Forts of Pennsylvania—Volume I*, 427.

morning complaining about the "ghostly goings-on" that kept them awake all night. However, there was one young man who decided to "tough it out" after encountering the ghost on his first night in the haunted room back in 1890.

Evan L. Jones had recently graduated from the Wyoming Seminary and was now teaching in one of the two schools that had been set up for students in Nanticoke. It was in the middle of the school year, and the ambitious graduate had decided to advance his career by "reading law" with a local attorney.

In those days an aspiring lawyer did not have to go to law school to be eligible to take the bar exam. He could serve as an attorney's understudy and take the exam once he felt he was qualified to do so. This was young Jones's intention, but the effort robbed him of his sleep, since he spent most of his nights poring over law books well into the early morning hours of the next day.

Despite his determination, however, there were some nights when his drowsy eyes would no longer stay open, and his brain refused to absorb any more facts. It was on one such evening that Evan finally had had enough and crawled into bed at midnight. Since he was mentally exhausted, he was soon fast asleep, his last thoughts being of torts and writs and other matters of jurisprudence.

He hadn't slept for more than an hour when he was awakened by a light in his room. Looking up at the ceiling light he was surprised to see it was turned off. His groggy mind struggled to comprehend that, but when he looked over to the side of the room opposite his bed, he saw an incandescent yellow orb that seemed to undulate and quiver as it grew in size.

Satisfied that the orb was the source of the light that had awakened him, the aspiring lawyer couldn't take his eyes off of it. Then, to his horror, the shimmering luminescence gradually shaped itself into the figure that he would later describe as that of a "gigantic Continental soldier with eyes like balls of fire!"

Since he wasn't a "drinking man," Jones knew he wasn't seeing things as a result of imbibing too much alcohol. In his half-awake state the only other explanation that came to mind was that he was dreaming, and so, being a logical and practical sort, he closed his eyes and rolled over onto his side so his back was now toward the light.

Nonetheless, the weird occurrence had flustered Jones, and despite his best efforts he could not fall asleep. Finally, in an attempt to convince himself that it was all just a nightmare after all, he opened his eyes once again. Then what he saw this time threw him into a panic.

There, standing right beside his bed, was the huge apparition staring down at him with its glowing eyes. Not knowing what else to do, the terror-stricken boarder grabbed for the on-off cord hanging from the electric light on the ceiling above the bed.

The old place had been one of the first in town to be electrified, and when the light went on this night the result was not only dramatic, but it also filled the young man with relief.

As soon as the bulb lit up, the strange specter seemed to dissolve into the soft yellow glow that filled the room. It didn't take much thought for the shaken sleeper to decide then and there that he'd leave the ceiling light on until morning.

However, the next morning Mrs. Jake Schappert, his fidgety landlady, reproved him for leaving the light burn and scolded him by noting "That's very wasteful, Mr. Jones!"

"I didn't sleep well. In fact, I had a fitful evening," came the tired young man's explanation.

Mrs. Schappert's reaction was one filled with remorse and surprise. "Oh my God, you didn't see it, did you?" she expostulated when she had had time to recover her wits. The old lady then asked her boarder to describe what he had seen, and once he had given a vivid account, she begged him not to tell anyone, because it would "ruin the reputation of the boarding house."

He magnanimously agreed to her wishes, and even stayed on for another month before finding other lodging. And in all that time he never saw the specter again. Whether or not anyone else did after that is not known today, but if they did then maybe Mrs. Schappert also convinced them not to talk about her ghost.

On the other hand, maybe someone saw the huge wraith with its menacing eyes and felt obligated to warn others about it, thereby putting the landlady out of business. Perhaps that old boarding house may still be standing there today, because, according to Evan Jones' son, "it has (since

The Wyoming Massacre Battle Monument. Wyomng, Luzerne County.

his father's encounter) recently been sided over," thereby giving it a more modern and inviting look.[18]

Although we don't know if Mrs. Schappert's boarding house is still standing, we do know that the incident at the nearby "bloody rock" was a real one and the blood of unfortunate captives once flowed freely over it. The events that occurred here were, in the words of noted Wyoming Valley historian George Peck, no "mere fancy" but "undoubted historical fact."[19]

Regardless of whether you believe the story or not, the rock is still there, and of all the valley's legends and folktales it is the story of the Bloody Rock

18. W. G. Jones (born 1905), interviewed February 2, 1974.
19. Peck, Ibid, 284–285.

that seems to be the tale that is most indelibly stamped upon the region. However, as some scholars have noted, it is at this spot where it might be said that folklore seems to have been hardest at work when turning its attention to the Battle of Wyoming.

Local imaginations were without doubt once stimulated by the fact that a portion of the infamous stone had a distinct reddish cast, enough so that it reminded more credulous onlookers of blood stains. Geologists say the red color is due to the ferrous content of this part of the rock, since iron tends to discolor in this way, but for generations the widespread belief was that the red color was there because the blood of Queen Esther's victims stained it this way.[20]

Today there are few of us who would believe that, especially since eradicable bloodstains on steps and floors are a fanciful feature of haunted manor houses and castles in the British Isles, with Holyrood Palace being one such example and Moretham Tower in Yorkshire being another.

The indelible stains on the spiral stairs in Moretham Tower, the ancient seat of the Rokeby family, are said to be drops of blood from the knife of one of the medieval lords of the manor when he stabbed his beautiful wife to death in a fit of jealous rage and then beheaded her.[21]

The poor woman's skull is said to lie at the bottom of the Tees, a lake near the manor house, but it has never been found, unlike skulls of some of the victims of the Wyoming Massacre. Buried with all victims' bones in a common vault under the Wyoming Massacre Battle Monument in the town of Wyoming, the skulls are proof of the way these early settlers died.

The historical markers here indicate that some of the skulls have bullet holes where musket balls entered the cranium and snuffed out a life, and others show both bullet holes and the deep grooves of the scalping knife, morbid reminders which show how much those settlers were willing to sacrifice in order to gain the freedom and independence we often take for granted today.

---

20. Ibid.
21. J. A. Brooks, *Britain's Haunted Heritage*, 162.

CHAPTER 11

DARK SIDE OF THE MOUNTAINS

Throughout the world there are locations where natural laws and scientific logic seem to be refuted by events that fly in the face of what has become the accepted norm. So outlandish are the occurrences at such spots, that they grab and hold peoples' attention, and the sites where they happen soon become identified in popular culture as places of mystery. Here in Pennsylvania, there are a number of such mysterious places, and the stories about them seem to cling most persistently to the mountainous districts than to other, less romantically inclined, areas of the state.

And, as might be expected, many of these bizarre locales have been mentioned at one time or another in the first six volumes of the *Pennsylvania Fireside Tales* series, but there are a few others that were not accorded that notoriety, and so in this chapter I've decided to include a few more of my favorites, starting with a place called Gravity Hill.

Gravity Hill is not unique, not even in Pennsylvania. There are places all over the world, and others here in the Keystone State as well, where it is claimed that the law of gravity seems to have been annulled. However, Gravity Hill, located along Bethel Hollow Road near the small village of New Paris in Bedford County, is one spot where, since it was relatively close, I could personally investigate those dubious claims and verify the odd way in which gravity's polarity seems to have been reversed.

Skeptics often condescendingly argue that the apparent contradiction of natural law that's observed at Gravity Hill, and other places just like it, is nothing more than a simple optical illusion; that the mind is duped by a subtle trick played upon us by Mother Nature. On the other hand, those who visit these locales and put them to the test aren't so easily convinced, and I have to admit I fell into this category once I tried some of my own experiments at the Bedford County mystery site; and this confession comes from someone trained to analyze situations using the scientific method.

Gravity Hill is off the beaten path and so it's not easy to find. However, directions to the odd place can be found on an Internet website where descriptions of what to expect once you're there are outlined as well. According to that information, visitors should try two things once they've come to this lonely spot.

The first suggested experiment is to drive to the bottom of the hill, place your car in neutral, take your foot off the brake, release the emergency brake, then sit back and prepare to be amazed. Within seconds the car begins to drift, but not in a forward motion. Contrary to all expectations, the vehicle begins to move in the opposite way, moving slowly uphill!

For anyone needing further proof that something odd is going on here, there is yet another experiment that can be done to clear the matter up, and to do so it is best to bring along a carpenter's level to check the "lay" of the land. I had forgotten to bring that one piece of laboratory equipment along on the day my wife and I visited here. Nonetheless, there was a Coca Cola bottle lying alongside the road, just where a careless litterbug had thrown it, and it was half-filled with water.

Thinking the dirty soda bottle would serve as a tolerable level, I laid it on the hill beside the road with the open end facing downhill, and, not surprisingly, much of the water drained out and flowed downward. Then I emptied out all of the liquid and laid the bottle down on the road with the mouth of the bottle facing the hillside beside the paved surface that climbed Gravity Hill.

Once I let go of it, the glass container began to move, but like the car, it took off in a direction that was baffling. It too rolled up the hill, rather than down![1]

Analytical and logical minds say the apparent upward roll in the case of both the car and the bottle can be explained by the fact that the slope of the land on which Gravity Hill rests is decidedly different than the slope of

---

1. www.gravityhill.com

By the Seven Switches. Pine-Loganton Road, Pine Mountain, Clinton County.

Gravity Hill. In other words, the overall downward slope of the larger site overrides the slight downward slope of the hill that is tilted the opposite way. As far as the validity of that theory when applied to Gravity Hill, I can only say that the land surrounding Gravity Hill would do the Flat Earth Society proud.

There is no apparent slope to the surrounding territory, and so no apparent reason why things tend to roll up rather than down the hill. Readers can always visit the place and decide for themselves, but there is another hillside spot in another part of the state that may be even more intriguing to those who would like to explore ghostly realms and solve an old murder mystery.

Tucked away in a secluded glen of the Bald Eagle Mountain, not far from where old Fort Horn once stood, near Pine Station, Clinton County, and along the little-traveled mountain road locals call the Pine-Loganton Road, there is a weathered hunting camp that was for many generations the homestead of the Simcox family.

Known for decades as guides and hunters, the Simcox brothers and their descendants were also keepers of the many old tales and legends that were once as plentiful on the mountain as the deer that drew nimrods from miles around during the hunting season. Although deer and members of the Simcox family might not be as plentiful through here as they once were, both can still be found in this vicinity, and it was a member of the Simcox family who passed on to me some of the annals of the area that make the Pine-Loganton Road a candidate for one of those spots people like to think of as mysterious places.

"Back then people on the mountain didn't want nothing to do with anyone else," said Bill Simcox. "My granddad used to say that people down in McElhatten were 'flatlanders,'" he reminisced. "It's just too bad you didn't come around thirty years ago when Grammy was here," bemoaned the Wayne Township resident on the fine spring day he passed the strange tales of the Pine-Loganton Road on to us.

"My grandmother, Sara Jane Simcox, was a real Christian," he went on, kind of validating the reliability of his sources for the tales he was about to tell us. "She read the family Bible. Every night that was her ritual before she'd go to bed.

"Now that Bible is this thick, with all the birthdates and all the kids right on back kept in it, and she read that Bible through twice! So, when I was a kid and she'd tell you something, I always believed her; she wouldn't lie! And my granddad, he was the kind of guy who never talked much about anything, but when he'd tell you something you knew it must be true too, you know.

"I'd sometimes stay with them out there (at the old Simcox homestead) overnight, and every now and then they'd get to talkin' about that stuff. Whenever Grammy would say something, then pap would join in, and they'd scare you a little bit!

"Grammy talked about old grandmother Throstle and how mean she was. She was wicked, into the Black Arts and stuff, and would kill cats by throwing them into wood stoves. But Grammy said that when grandmother Throstle died, they had an awful time with her! She was screamin' and hollerin' about the cats. 'Get those cats away from me', over and over!

"But the Throstles never got along with their neighbors, the McClures, and Grammy said that grandmother Throstle, I guess about a year before she died, went out through the apple orchard that was there at the time, and laid her hand on every one of those trees and said, 'Those damn McClures will never get an apple off any of those trees!'[2]

The old witch's curse apparently was a powerful one, or at least there would have been many mountain folks around at that time that would have believed so, because all the trees seemed to lose the ability to produce any apples after the old hex placed her spell on them.

In the spring when other apple trees had produced beautiful white blossoms, the trees in the McClure orchard were colorless, seemingly stripped of their springtime flowers by strong gusts of wind. It was a condition often noted by the life-long resident of Pine Station who was recalling the tale to us.

"That always fascinated me, because when I was a kid the orchard was still there and the trees were good trees," he observed. "But no apples; there never was no apples on them!"[3]

Over the years the cursed orchard became a place where few dared to tread, and some of the old peoples' claims, that they saw the devil walking through it one night, sealed its fate as a place to avoid altogether. Not one of the gnarled trees bore any fruit as years went by, the old witch's curse apparently holding fast even after the passage of many decades. Then finally, not too many years ago, the sterile forest was bulldozed to clear more ground around the Simcox hunting camp.

Today, of course, we'd say some sort of natural blight was the cause of the apple trees' failure to produce apples. Back then, however, Mrs. Throstle's contemporaries would have given more credence to supernatural explanations than to "high-falutin" scientific ideas. That certainly would also have been the case with one of the weirdest spook stories I've yet documented; a narrative known along the Pine-Loganton Road as the story of the dancing cupboard.

Probably the most well-known account of that tale was the version documented in a series of newspaper articles that appeared in the *Clinton County Weekly* of Lock Haven, between May 4, 1934, and March 15, 1935. The location of the strange episode that was described in some detail in the newspaper was set at a place along the Pine-Loganton road known locally as the "Seven Switches."

---

2. Bill Simcox (born April 24, 1934), recorded January 9, 2000.
3. Ibid.

Along the Millheim-Siglerville Pike. Taken in Greenbriar Gap, Big Poe Mountain, Centre County. Rear view of the old schoolhouse (now Clover Hunting Camp) at the entrance to the field that is haunted by the Ingleby Monster.

Located near the highest point on the road, the Switches got its name from events that occurred here during the area's lumbering heyday. It seems that during that period, which lasted from 1880 up until about 1900, the dirt road on the mountaintop would become saturated with rainwater in the spring of the year. The heavy rains softened the road to the point where it became heavily rutted as teamsters passed through with their heavy wagonloads of logs.

In order to avoid the ruts, the waggoners would drive to firmer ground beside the muddier path, and this new route would be followed until it, too, became rutted. Then waggoners would switch over to a more navigable path beside the second "switch," and this would continue until eventually there were seven switches that were created over the years.

None of those switches can be seen today, the area is now heavily overgrown with trees; and few locals can even recall where the switches were located, and that they were once such a prominent feature on the mountain. Likewise, few recall that it was here one night in 1904, that a local lad would have an experience he would never forget.

The young beau, according to the version of the tale related in the newspaper, had been visiting his girlfriend's farmhouse on the Sugar Valley side of the mountain. His visit had been a pleasant one, and as all good things must come to an end, he was headed back up the Pine-Loganton Road to his parent's farmstead at the foot of the north face of the Bald Eagle Mountain, near Pine Station.

It was a bright moonlit night, and the love-struck teenager's thoughts must have only been on the pleasant evening he had just had, but those nice mental pictures quickly evaporated when an unusual object suddenly appeared on the road ahead, just as he came to the Seven Switches. It was not something he expected to see in this lonely place, particularly at this time of night, but there it was, with its contents gleaming brightly in the moonlight.

At first, he was transfixed by the site of the old-fashioned cupboard and its elegant china visible through the windows of the cupboard's doors. The glazed porcelain dishes, radiant with many different bright colors, were arranged neatly in rows, and were supported by racks so they stood on their edges for optimum viewing. There were even lacy white curtains with tie-backs of red ribbon behind the windows, and they added an even more refined touch to the presentation. Nonetheless, despite the beauty of the nicely-finished wooden cupboard and its contents, it was all soon forgotten when it began to "dance."

First it jumped to one side of the road, then to the other, then backward and then forward, always staying some little distance ahead of its lone observer. It was such an unnerving experience that the young mountain man found he could not run; and he was also upset by the fact that no matter how fast he walked, the cupboard kept between him and a clear passage to the safety of his home.

Then to his horror the cupboard seemed to grow arms, which extended outward as though they were trying to grab him. The cupboard continued its dance, but when it made a quick jump toward him it was the final straw; it gave the terrified teen the surge of adrenalin he needed to make his getaway.

Taking off as fast as he could run, the horrified boy still could not get around his nemesis. It tauntingly danced ahead of him, always between him and the refuge of his home. Then, in his rush, he tripped, and at the same time the cupboard seemed to do so also, falling to the ground with a crash that sounded "as though it had been hurled to a cobblestone street from a fourth-story window."

Dishes spilled out onto the road and rolled all around the fallen lad, who tried to run again. He was, however, unable to stand up at first, crawling on hands and knees for about sixty yards before he was finally able to get to his feet and make a final dash for home.

Once there, the terrified runner flung himself against the door of his house, which gave way and caused him to fall headlong onto the front hallway. His unheralded entrance was surprising enough to the occupants of the homestead, but when they saw the condition of the breathless boy's clothes and the scrapes and scratches on his body, they were even more perplexed.

It took some time for the winded lad to calm down enough to explain to his parents what had happened, but when he did so his father seemed to have an explanation for the strange apparition that had frightened his son so badly. It was, claimed the man, a manifestation of a valley servant girl who had been murdered at the Seven Switches about twenty-five years earlier.[4]

Today, locals know nothing about the supposed murder of a local mountain maid at the Seven Switches, nor can they recall any details about the dancing cupboard that some once thought was her ghostly manifestation. On the other hand, just seven years ago Bill Simcox still remembered his grandparents talking about it, and their accounts seemed to coincide with the newspaper story's details.

"My granddad used to say about the cupboard dancing on the road over there. He said there were certain times of the year that people would be driving their buggies through there and this damn cupboard would come out and bounce up and down the road, and the dishes rattled inside! Now Granpap never said he saw it, but different people said they'd seen it. They certainly talked about it back then."

Then it became obvious that our narrator had his own theory about the matter. "You know they all had kerosene lamps back then, and I think a lot

---

4. Homer Tope Rosenberger, *Mountain Folks*, 90–95.

of that stuff stems from not being able to see at night," he proposed. "You heard a strange noise and looked quick to see what it was!"[5]

It seemed like a tidy logical way to end my narrative of the dancing cupboard; just explain it away as a figment of peoples' imaginations. However, seven years later I was to form a different opinion when I started to write this chapter and decided to call my original informant to clarify some details on his strange account. I was crestfallen when his wife answered the telephone and explained to me that her husband had recently "passed away."

But then my spirits were buoyed, when she helpfully noted that her mother-in-law was yet alive, with her mental faculties still unimpaired at age eighty-seven. Moreover, the elderly lady's daughter-in-law thought her mother-in-law would probably be more than happy to answer my questions.

I wasted no time in calling the life-long resident of Pine Mountain, and Edna Simcox was all her daughter-in-law had promised. She was not only affable, but she had clear recollections of the people and stories of the Pine-Loganton Road, including the tales she heard her mother-in-law, Sara Jane Simcox, relate many times; and one of those episodes was the tale of the dancing cupboard.

Sara Jane, born in 1886, and her husband, Hallie Simcox, lived along the Pine-Loganton Road for most of their lives, and when she died at age seventy-two Sara Jane was one of the older residents living up on the mountain at the time. As such, Sara's accounts of her early days at this remote spot were avidly listened to by her friends, neighbors, and family, and among those family members was Sara Jane's daughter-in-law Edna.

Sara Jane's narratives left a vivid impression on Edna's mind, but the one that seems to have impressed her the most was Sara's account of how one evening she was walking along the Pine-Loganton Road and saw the dancing cupboard at the Seven Switches.

She was by herself at the time, and perplexed by the event, but the details of her strange encounter seem to have been forgotten. Today Sara Jane's daughter-in-law, who heard Sara Jane relate the story firsthand, cannot recall any specifics. However, she does remember that this devout Bible-reading mountain lady always ended her account with the statement that "You can believe, 'cause I seen it!"[6]

---

5. Bill Simcox, Ibid.
6. Edna Simcox (born 1919), interviewed January 14, 2007.

Those who profess not to believe in these kinds of things today would still say that the mind can play profound tricks and cause us to see things that aren't really there at all. It's an explanation that satisfies us and makes us feel more comfortable with the world around us. It's also the reason, many would profess, that no one sees the dancing cupboard along the Pine-Loganton Road anymore.

We have advanced, they would say, beyond the place where we can be as easily fooled as some of the less scientifically-enlightened folks of seventy or more years ago. However, some of the locals along the Pine-Loganton Road may argue about that, saying that the spirit of the young girl who was murdered at the Seven Switches may have tired of manifesting itself as a dancing cupboard and decided to make its presence known in a different way, before "giving up the ghost" entirely.

Sightings of the cupboard seemed to gradually die off with the old folks who once lived on the mountain. Eventually no one reported seeing it anymore, but then in the 1940s the old story surfaced once again, when

The haunted field. Along the Millheim-Siglerville Pike, this field is said to be the haunt of a local fiend that is referred to in local folklore as The Ingleby Monster.

people began to hear what sounded like a woman's screams coming from a level area on the mountain about a half mile below the Seven Switches.

Old-timers once referred to the flat near the Simcox camp as The Golden Thread Patch, and why they did so is not recalled anymore. On the other hand, the dreadful screams that seemed to originate there and which sounded like a woman calling out for help over and over again still ring in the ears of those who heard them.

The chilling shrieks would start in the evening, just as it was getting dark, and they seemed to occur more frequently in the fall than during other times of the year. Their human-like quality left little doubt in peoples' minds that they came from the throat of a desperate young woman, but others, who either had not experienced them for themselves or who were not willing to admit of otherworldly things, said the cries were nothing more than animal sounds. Despite their differences, however, neither believers nor non-believers wanted to take the next step and investigate the mystery firsthand.

It just didn't seem like a very inviting thing to do, no matter how intriguing the mystery, to wind your way down through the darkening forest and out onto the lonely flat where no one knew what awaited them. And so, like the sightings of the dancing cupboard, reports of the strange sounds declined over time too, and no one in recent years has even claimed to have heard them. Nevertheless, there are some who might argue that those who are in the right place at the right time might still detect the same blood-curdling shrieks yet today.

However, the question that then naturally arises is whether those folks would be more likely or less inclined to investigate the intimidating noises than folks of sixty years ago. Perhaps they, too, would decide that it was just too scary, and that they had better things to do, even if it meant a damsel in distress would have no hero to rescue her from her plight.[7]

It would not be an unexpected reaction. Many folks have experienced strange events and occurrences in similar areas of the Pennsylvania hills; remote and lonely spots where, even on the sunniest days, there is an unexplained feeling of dread or uneasiness that seems to well up in the breast of anyone who ventures into them. And of all these mysterious places, I would like to mention one more; a place that, many once believed, is the home of a creature known as the Ingleby Monster.

7. Edna Simcox, Ibid.

Once hailed as "Centre County's foremost resort town," the tiny settlement of Ingleby was also known for its bees, which, some say, were actually the basis for its name. It seems that an early settler named Ingle kept beehives here as a livelihood, and there are those who believe Ingle and his bees were the inspiration for the naming of the village.[8]

However, over the years Ingleby has also achieved some notoriety for its monster, or the story of its monster, even though there does seem to be debate about whether or not the whole tale is anything more than a fabrication. Folks who grew up in Ingleby say they never heard anything about a monster around there, until their kids brought the story home after hearing it from their classmates.

For now, an exploration of the truth behind the tale can wait. Let us just present the story in the way that it was probably told and retold in hushed tones of wonderment by students, when they passed it on to friends in the halls and classrooms of Penns Valley High School.

The setting for the doleful tale was an old farmhouse, that once stood in a lonesome clearing, located somewhere in the hills that surround the little community of Ingleby in Penn Township of Centre County. Although the barn had collapsed by then, the deserted house was still standing about fifty years ago.

Ravaged by time, its windows were gone, and it was not much more than a shell, so that today there is probably not much left except a crumbling foundation. To those who saw it fifty years ago there was a decidedly weathered and wearied look about the place, as though its abandonment was not a recent one, and in fact that was the case. At least that's what was claimed in the local story that told of the horrible events that once supposedly occurred here sometime during the last decade of the nineteenth century or first decade of the twentieth.

Back then, in the days when the railroad came through the town and there was a hotel to accommodate vacationers who came to be reinvigorated by the fresh country air, it was a routine custom for many locals to go into the larger neighboring communities on Saturday nights to do their shopping and socializing. Saturday nights, therefore, meant the folks of Ingleby, and those who lived in the surrounding hollows, could often be found in the nearby villages of Coburn or Millheim enjoying their one and

8. Paul M. Dubbs, *Where-to-go and Place Names of Centre County*, 71.

only night on the town for the week. And among the regulars was the family who lived in the house that seemed so far back in the woods; considered remote even in that sparsely settled age.

Neighbors here in those days were scarce, and so everyone looked out for one another in a general spirit of cooperation and mutual support. As a result, if a family failed to come to town on a Saturday night their absence was noted by someone; and so it was, that on one Saturday night the absence of the hill hawks who lived out on the mountain was duly noted and often mentioned in passing conversations. However, when the family failed to show up on the following Saturday night and then again on the next one, it was decidedly not a good sign, so people agreed they should see if something was wrong.

When they got to the secluded homestead there was no one there, even though the table was set for the evening meal with dishes of food on the table. Since the food had not been touched, it appeared that the family had been frightened away by something before they could sit down to their dinner. It seemed apparent that they had fled in such haste, in fact, that they hadn't left a clue as to where they were going. It was a mystery that was never solved, and for several years the homestead remained unoccupied.

Then, unexpectedly one day, a stranger took up residence there. He was not a local and he seemed to like his privacy, but his neighbors tried to befriend him anyway, stopping by once in a while to say hello. Then one day when someone went in to speak to him, they found his beheaded body on the cabin floor. That, too, remained an unsolved mystery, at least according to the tale, but for the country folks of the area it was the proverbial last straw.

"Stories started racing through the valley that there was some kind of evil force or monster at Ingleby," recalled the valley resident who had heard the old tale when, as a teenager, he had worked as a night watchman at nearby Poe Valley State Park. "And over time this evil force, or whatever it was, supposedly became invisible," he went on.

"Now the monster supposedly haunts a copse of trees that stands across a field in back of where the old schoolhouse used to be, and I don't know if it's still there, along the right side of the first road out of Coburn into Poe Valley [the Millheim-Siglerville Pike]. Now I'll tell you one thing. You know how your mind can play tricks, well I went in there with four or five

The Coburn Railroad Tunnel. Crossing the railroad bridge across Penns Creek here takes you into the haunts of the Ingleby Monster. Fisherman used to avoid this spot come nightfall!

other guys one night about forty years ago, and I thought it was particularly dark in there!"[9]

His uncanny nocturnal experience turned out not to be the only one, nor, as it turned out, the strangest one, that our narrator was going to leave us with, as regards the Ingleby Monster. It was near this copse of trees, he would go on to say, that a friend of his was scared out of his wits one day during hunting season back in the early 1960s. Several years later, that same friend willingly related his strange experience to the writer of these lines when I called him to verify the story.

He was about twelve or thirteen, back in 1960 or 1961, when he had gone hunting in the mountains above Ingleby and Coburn. It was early October, during small game season, and it was just starting to get dark when the teenager came out of the dark recesses of Stillhouse Hollow about a half mile from the old country schoolhouse.

The solitary hunter was not uncomfortable about being alone in the woods, particularly while carrying a rifle, and so he was not unnerved when he thought he sensed, more than heard, something on the dirt road behind

9. Jeffry Wert (born 1946), recorded July 23, 1997, telephone interview January 26, 2007.

him. He turned and looked, but there was nothing there, and so he started out again. For a while it seemed as though it had been his imagination, but when the sensation returned, only more strongly this time, he became concerned.

He had the distinct and unpleasant impression that whatever or who-ever was behind him was closing in fast, and it may have been at that moment when an admonition came to mind; a warning he had heard more than once over the years. One of his favorite pastimes growing up here was listening to the oldest men in the area as they loafed and swapped tales in Coburn's country store.

He had especially liked their hunting and fishing stories, and one of the adages often proffered by the fisherman was that "You never go fishing down by the old railroad tunnel [near Coburn and Ingleby] after dark." When pressed for details they would decline to talk about the matter any further, so whether it was the old tales that were causing his imagination to work overtime or whether it was just because he was tired, the excited teen was now convinced that there had to be someone following him.

He stopped and turned around a second time, determined to keep looking until he spotted his silent stalker. Just as before, however, he again saw no trace of a mysterious follower. Then all of a sudden, he experienced a cold chill spreading over his entire body and an unpleasant clammy sen-sation that almost felt like someone was trying to take hold of him.

The feeling was overpowering, and thoughts of small game were for-gotten as the frightened hunter ran, in his words, "at a high rate of speed," out of the area. He says he's been back now that he's older, but for many years after his hair-raising experience he avoided this place of mystery, an area that local folktales say may still be haunted by the Ingleby Monster.[10]

The tale of the Ingleby Monster still causes people in Penns Valley to pause and wonder if any parts of it are true. Accounts of up-close and personal encounters, like that of the young hunter, are often explained away as imaginations gone wild. However, an explanation like this in the case of the young hunter is not one that is acceptable to the man he has become today. "I know what I felt in there," he says, and I used to be teased a lot about it by my friends. But no one ever accepted my offer to come get them if they went back there alone to check it out for themselves!"[11]

---

10. Verne Jodon (born 1948), interviewed January 26, 2007.
11. Ibid.

Today our pragmatic society requires that the more fantastic the claims, the more stringent the evidence should be, that proves the validity of the claims. Or in the words of astrophysicist Carl Sagan, "Extraordinary claims require extraordinary proof."

Certainly, one thing that could be done to find out if there are threads of truth woven into the tale of the Ingleby Monster is to scour old newspaper accounts to see if there is a record of a Penn Township family's disappearance around the time the Ingleby Monster story says they vanished, or whether a murder occurred here at the same time. Such an exercise would be a time- consuming chore, and most probably a fruitless one.

It would seem, therefore, that for now it's safe to say that the Ingleby Monster will remain as elusive as Bigfoot. Not exactly a nice solution to our little mystery, but an apt comparison, if there is any truth to the claim that not too many years ago someone did spot a Bigfoot-like ape sitting on one of the high ledges that frown down upon the silent little village from which its alleged monster may have taken its name.

CHAPTER 12

WOLF TALES FROM THE DEEP WOODS

Those who have read the other six volumes in my *Pennsylvania Fireside Tales* series will have some knowledge about the habits and characteristics of Pennsylvania's early wolf packs. That they were nocturnal by nature and cowardly during the day is a well-documented fact.

Likewise, they proved to be cowardly when acting alone, but as a pack driven by hunger, they would attack any beast and any traveler unfortunate enough to be caught out in the woods alone after dark.

Nothing could be more terrifying to such a traveler than the howls of a wolf pack closing in around them for the kill, especially if no apparent means of escape was evident, other than climbing the nearest tree and waiting it out until morning.

Many such men were once forced to do just that, and the snarls and growls of the beasts on the ground below were as chilling to them as the war whoop of the Indian was to their ancestors. In either case, however, it was a sound not soon forgotten; but in the cases of the wolf attacks, those in the trees would always be gazing down at multiple sets of glowing yellow eyes and flashing white fangs instead of at painted warriors. The color of the wolves' coats, on the other hand, would vary, apparently depending upon in which part of the state the events occurred.

In the eastern and central parts of Pennsylvania the wolf was usually brown in color, but as you moved further west their color was more likely to be grey, until in the westernmost parts there were, as Moravian missionary John Heckewelder wrote in 1818, "more black than grey wolves."[1]

That there were many large wolf packs during those early times is well documented as well, so it's not surprising that there are many accounts that surface yet today about how people's ancestors were hounded by these ferocious predators. Such episodes have been preserved in almost all Pennsylvania counties, but they are getting harder and harder to find, and it's for this reason that I've decided to preserve a few of these "dying breeds" in the pages that follow.

So here are tales of those early times that show how bold and fearless both predator and prey could be during some of Pennsylvania's wildest years; accounts that tell of wolf threats and attacks, and the steps people took to deal with them or to hunt down the perpetrators.

Some of the stories come from documented sources, but others come from people I've been fortunate enough to interview during the last several years; the descendants of those who lived during those chilling times when wolf packs roamed freely throughout the mountains and valleys of this fair state.

Starting in the western county of Westmoreland, there is a tale from Unity Township, in the heart of that county, that tells of a typical wolf encounter in that section sometime in 1801 or 1802.

Early Westmoreland County settler Christian Shockey had been hunting all day, and the night was turning cold as he made his way back home. In the distance behind him he suddenly heard the howls of a wolf pack, which pursued him for several miles as he made his way through the thickness of a darkening forest.

The pack finally got close enough that he could have shot one with the musket he always carried with him when entering the woods, but he realized that killing only one of the beasts would not deter the rest. He then decided that his best bet was to gain safety by climbing the nearest tree, and, spotting an ancient white pine along the trail ahead, he soon affected his escape.

Shockey spent an anxious night in his perch, listening to the howls of the wolves directly below him all night, and being treated to the sounds of their snapping jaws and the raking noise of their claws as they jumped

1. John Heckewelder, letter written to Peter S. Du Pouceau, dated August 12, 1818.

The wolf-haunted forest in Henry's Valley. View of woods along Laurel Run in Henry's Valley, Perry County.

onto the tree trunk in their efforts to climb up and snatch their prey from his precarious haven.

This assault continued until daylight, at which time the wolves skulked off to their dens, allowing Shockey to climb down and make his way safely home. It was said that for many years afterwards the bark of the tree where Shockey took his refuge bore the claw and teeth marks of the wolves. In the end, however, Shockey got his revenge as time passed.

His cabin was located near a large spring that was notable because it never froze over in the wintertime. The open waters of the warm spring provided an easy water source year-round, and the wolves were frequent imbibers. Taking note of that fact, Shockey exacted his retribution on the animals. He would eventually sell the hides of hundreds of them that he caught in the many steel traps he set up around the spring. Consequently, for many years afterwards, and maybe even today, the spring was referred to as the Wolf Spring.[2]

---

2. John N. Boucher, *History of Westmoreland County, Pennsylvania,* 208–33.

A similar tale from Lycoming County reveals yet another way a lone nocturnal traveler defended himself from a hungry wolf pack. The gentleman in this case was one of the first settlers along Larry's Creek in that county. Peter Duffy had built his cabin near the mouth of the creek in 1784, as had several others at some distance away.

The area was a wilderness at that time and the only way through it was along an old Indian path which served as a link between the widely-separated cabins. One night in 1795, as he and his horse made their way along the path after visiting one of his neighbors, Duffy was assailed by a pack of ravenous wolves. He had not brought his musket along, and as a last resort he grabbed a stout stick which he used as a cudgel to successfully fight off the wolves until morning.

Although Duffy made it back home safely, the assault took its toll on the brave pioneer. Shortly afterwards, probably due to the shock and stress of the attack and the exposure to the cold weather of that evening, he contracted a cold which led to a violent fever and eventual death. The place where the attack occurred was referred to at that time as the "Big Glen," and two hundred years later it was yet being described as "still a gloomy place."[3]

Today the spot, near Mount Zion Church in Brady Township, Lycoming County, remains somewhat off the beaten path and is as overgrown with thick brush and tall timber as it must have been in Duffy's day.

Bradford County seems to have been a favorite hangout for ravenous wolf packs during the early 1800s as well. Something young Slim West found out the hard way one night after leaving his father's home to trek two miles through the Towanda Hills to visit a neighbor.

He had only gone a short distance before a pack of gray wolves picked up his scent and began to follow him. Soon the woods echoed with their melancholy chorus as they slowly closed in on their intended victim.

They would've eventually caught him, except for a neighbor's cabin that sat along his pathway. No one was at the Cox homestead when he reached it, and so the frightened young man barged through the front door and rapidly climbed the ladder leading to the upper story. After getting to the second floor, he judiciously pulled the ladder up after him just as the howling wolves filled the room below.

---

3. John F. Meginness, *History of Lycoming County, Pennsylvania*, 672.

They maintained their malicious vigil and kept up their dreadful howling until the first rays of daylight began to penetrate the thick canopy of the surrounding forest, at which time they slinked away to their rocky dens in the surrounding hollows. Once they were gone, West lost no time in returning home, where he related his hair-raising story.[4]

In that same county, in its earliest period of settlement, there lived a family named Ingham who also had to deal with wolves. John Ingham and his wife Miranda were among the first settlers at Camptown, near present-day Wyalusing, and it's from that family that I've collected an episode that's as close to a Little Red Riding Hood type tale that I've ever found in Pennsylvania's legends and lore.

The Ingham's six-year-old daughter had spent the day visiting relatives, and it was nearly dark when she had to make her way back home through what was then a thick virgin forest. It's hard for us today to believe that parents would let a six-year-old make such a dangerous trip alone. Nonetheless, that's what happened, and on her way the little girl met what she thought at first was her father's dog on the trail ahead.

She spoke to the animal, but it ignored her and quickly disappeared back into the woods. Shortly afterwards there came a howl from deep within those woods, and it was immediately answered by a number of other howls which came from all around her. The innocent young child then realized her predicament.

Although she had at first thought the animal she had encountered was her father's dog, she recalled that it was the same size and color as a wolf. That realization, coupled with the knowledge of the woods and its wildlife she had learned from her parents, spurred her to action. The unearthly howls, she decided, were those of wolves that had surrounded her, and she took off running as fast as she could go.

In the meantime, her uncle Joseph had heard the wolves as well, and, fearing for his little niece's life, he mounted his horse and took off in a gallop to find her. Much to his relief he caught up with her just as she was arriving home safely. It's recalled that she was not only out of breath, but also "sadly frightened."[5]

Given the prevalence of attacks just like those related, it's no wonder that Pennsylvania's early settlers wanted to either scare wolves away whenever

---

4. Clement F. Heverly, *Pioneer and Patriot Families of Bradford County*, 220.
5. Reverend David Craft, *History of Bradford County, Pennsylvania*, 264.

possible, or kill them whenever they could. To be sure, historical records reveal many of the measures devised to drive off wolf packs or kill them whenever they assailed settlers' cabins at night or hassled people and their livestock. One such account, again from Bradford County, recalls how dogs were oftentimes one of the primary forms of defense against wolf marauders.

Ira Ballard, who was raised in a log cabin near present-day Mount Pisgah, was fond of recalling how large packs of wolves would gather around his cabin each night and "make us frantic with their terrible howls." Tiring of the commotion one evening, the family decided to let the family dog out in hopes that it would chase away the wolves. It was not a good decision, recalled the old homesteader, because when they found the dog later, all that was left of him was "a couple of ears and a few picked bones!"[6]

An account preserved by the great Moravian missionary John Heckewelder reveals yet another measure that had to be taken to protect horses from wolf attacks in the mountains of Bedford County in 1762. On March 30th of that year, he and a party of missionaries were crossing Bedford County's Allegheny Mountain, when, "after a hard day's journey" through three and a half feet of snow they reached a place called "Edmonds Swamp," near the summit of the mountain. Here they decided to spend the night in the cabin of a local hunter named "Saucy Jack" Miller.

"As soon as nightfall came on," relates Heckewelder, "the wolves put in their appearance and raised their dismal howl," which, he claimed, "was the night music of the place all the year round." He goes on to relate how Miller had no stable at his homestead, and so to protect the horses of travelers staying with him, Miller and his sons "kept watch all through the night."[7]

Pioneer hunter of Pennsylvania's Black Forest, Philip Tome, described a similar situation that occurred one evening during one of his many hunting trips. "At night I was surrounded by wolves, which frightened the horses by their howlings so that they came close to the fire. I tied them near the fire, fearing they might become so frightened as to break away and run home."[8]

The first settler on Nittany Mountain, beside the quaint mountain village of Pleasant Gap, Centre County, was also serenaded by the nocturnal howls of wolf packs that ruled the wilds of this area in the late 1700s.

---

6. Clement F. Heverly, *History and Geography of Bradford County, Pennsylvania*, 471.
7. Reverend Edward Rondthaler, *Life of John Heckewelder*, 39.
8. Philip Tome, *Pioneer Life*, 42.

The Big Glen at Mt. Zion Church. "Still a gloomy place" today, and where a ravenous wolf pack once attacked unsuspecting travelers—Brady Township, Lycoming County.

Michael Swaney's cabin sat near what later would become the railroad line that connected the nearby White Rock quarrying operations with the main line.

In Swaney's day the forest surrounding his isolated cabin was still virgin timberland, and home to wild animals of all types, including wolves. According to tales handed down through succeeding generations of his family, Swaney felt obliged on many occasions "to drive the wolves from his door at night."[9]

It's not recalled what method the old settler in the previous tale used to scare off the wolves that interrupted his sleep every night, but from a story handed down through generations of one Perry County family and from another preserved by descendants of early settlers in Northumberland County we can perhaps make an educated guess.

Born in 1860, "Uncle Jesse" Shaeffer was a native of Shaeffer's Valley in Perry County. Regaled as an avid hunter, the old-time lumberman was

9. Myrtle Magargle, "History of Pleasant Gap—First Installment," State College, PA, *Centre Daily Times*, March 16, 1936.

also known as a veritable treasure house of tales about the wolves that once made Shaeffer's Valley and nearby Henry's Valley their home.

Among those types of stories the hale and hearty pioneer was fond of telling was the one about how his grandmother Neidigh, who lived in Henry's Valley between Laurel Run and Bower Mountain, always kept a chestnut fence rail burning in the fireplace when the men folk went off to evening church services

"When the wolves came too close to the house," Uncle Jesse would recall, "she would open the door and shake the burning end of the rail at them." "This would," he asserted, "frighten them away, as they hated the sight of the fire."

"I recall when old man Haney's little girls were returning home with their fire basket," he would say when telling yet another Shaeffer's Valley wolf tale. "A light was carried in a fire basket from house to house to make fires in those days," he would explain, "and on this day the wolves appeared just as the girls were crossing the foot-log over the Yellow Belly or Terrapin Swamp, and they fell in, extinguishing the fire! Their clothes were ruined and with no fire they were afraid to go home!"[10]

The claim that use of fire was a technique used by early settlers to scare away wolves is also supported by a Centre County episode that occurred during the earliest part of the nineteenth century in Spring Township near present-day Bellefonte. One of the earliest settlers of the area at that time, when it was still mostly uncleared land, was Thomas McClellan.

His homestead in that dismal dense forest was often beset by wolf packs. The packs were so bold, it is recorded, that "he had to build fires to keep the wolves from his cabin, and even then the wolves would sometimes howl all night at the cabin's very door!"[11]

In the Schwaben Creek Valley of Northumberland County there was once another family who also had to deal with the nightly nuisance of wolf packs. "Packs of wolves would come close to their farmhouse every night, and howl very loud" recalled ninety-six-year-old Parsett Snyder, who heard the story from his grandmother Elmira Trautman.

Her parents, a family named Heintzelman, lived near the village of Leck Kill around 1855, and they were plagued by packs of wolves that

10. Author Unknown, "Wolf Days in Perry County," Newport PA, *Perry Review Volume 14, 1989*, The Perry Historians, 38.

11. Linn, *History of Centre and Clinton Counties*, 433.

would come down off Line Mountain every night to raid the Heintzelman chicken house and sheep pen.

At first, they were undecided as to how best manage the problem. However, through trial and error, the Heintzelmans learned that the most effective way to deal with it was to sacrifice the cured hams they had hanging in their smoke house. It was a bit of an economic hardship to do so, but it would have been even more expensive to lose their livestock to the wolves every night.

So as a sort of peaceful accommodation, the Heintzelmans threw pieces of their cured hams to the wolves when they got too close for comfort. The wolves would pounce on the delicious morsels and carry them off into the woods, leaving the Heintzelmans and their livestock safe for one more night.[12]

That their tactics were probably smart ones is supported by yet another account from northern Pennsylvania. Here, in 1873, it was reported that a ravenous wolf was ranging the hemlock forests of eastern Potter County and killing sheep over a wide area every night. Known as the "lone wolf," it was hard to track down. Consequently, the sheep kills continued until 1874 when a large black wolf, thought to be the same one, was shot between the waters of Phoenix and Pine Creeks.[13]

Other tales about how hunters gunned down the wolves over time, in order to collect the bounties offered for the hides, imply that this over-hunting led to the extermination of the wolves in the state. However, there were other factors that may have led to the wolf's demise as well, including poisoning, and hydrophobia (rabies) contracted from dogs. Regardless of the reason for their disappearance, we are fortunate to have been left with tales like these in this chapter that preserve a record of those times from the distant past.

12. Parsett Snyder (born 1919), interviewed April 30, 2013, and June 11, 2013.
13. J. H. Beers and Co., *History of McKean, Elk, Cameron and Potter Counties, Pennsylvania*, 1000.

CHAPTER 13

THE WILD MAN OF KOHLER VALLEY

One of the greatest pleasures I have had in collecting and writing about Pennsylvania's folktales and legends are the unexpected phone calls I get from those who want to share their stories with me. I received one such call one evening on a cold leaden-gray fall day back in 2013, and the tale proved to be one of the strangest I had yet heard in my quest for these gems of the forest which I had always sought.

The young lady who called had been hesitant to do so, entreating me several times to not "think she was crazy." I assured her that I had heard many unusual tales over the years, and that I had developed a realization that there is more to this world than meets the eye; that we should all keep an open mind about what's real and what's not. Somewhat assured by those words, my caller launched into her unusual tale.

"My father has a camp way back in Kohler Valley in the Seven Mountains country of Centre and Mifflin Counties," she began, "and when I was ten years old, he taught me to fish in the stream near the cabin. He had an unusual way of baiting the hook by using both a worm and a kernel of canned corn, so when I went fishing, I always carried a can of worms and a can of corn with me.

"One day in early fall of 1971 when I was ten years old, I was at the camp with my parents and grandparents, and I told them that I was going to take my fishing rod and go down to the nearby creek and fish for brown trout.

"Dad had always told me not to let the fish see me when I was fishing, because if they saw me, it would scare them away, so I always tried to hide myself somewhat in bushes along the stream wherever I fished. So, I came to the creek and first crossed to the other side before starting to fish. I had my worms in my bait can and some kernels of corn, and, since it was easier to fish this way, I dumped some of it on the ground before sitting down.

"After fishing for a while and getting no bites, I got up and moved downstream. Here I poured out more worms and corn kernels onto a little pile and then sat down to fish. I got no bites here either, so I moved on again.

"It was not a good day for fishing as I got no bites anywhere, despite moving on downstream two more times. Each time I stopped I always poured out a little pile of my bait on the bank of the stream before sitting down.

"After a while I got bored since the fish weren't biting, and so I decided to take a little walk. I walked up the hill behind me since I knew there was an old logging road up there that led to Barb Markey's camp, and I remember that the ferns on the hill were waist high until I got to the road. Once I got up to the road I started walking, and in about 10 minutes I came to a clearing.

"Much to my surprise, since I didn't expect to see anything like it in such a remote area, I saw an old brick ranch house with a dilapidated-looking one-story wooden shed to its left, and an old rusty car sitting on concrete blocks.

"I'm not sure what kind of car it was, but it reminded me of a Chevy Bel Air from the 1940s or 1950s. Sitting there also was an old doghouse where there was a shabby-looking dog tied up to it; it looked to be a German Shepherd/Labrador mix.

"I didn't want to intrude so I decided to walk on, taking extra care not to walk on the yard around the house so as to avoid trespassing, but as I moved away, I just had to look back. When I did, I could see what looked like an old woman, she had a small frame and white hair, standing inside at one of the windows.

"It seemed like it must have been a kitchen window since she never looked up and looked at me; she kept looking down like she was washing dishes. Outside that same window was a flower box under the window. It was white but the paint on it was peeling. There were flowers in it, but I don't remember what kind or color they were.

"As I stood there looking, an older man of average weight and height with white hair and no beard came running out the front door. He was wearing a pair of old bib overalls and was holding a large cane or walking stick in both hands while waving it around over his head in a threatening way.

"As I think back, it must have been a walking stick since it looked like all the bark had been whittled off of it so that it was bare, and it was a foot taller than a cane would have been. Anyway, he ran right towards me while screaming 'Get off this property' and swearing at me.

"I was absolutely terrified, and I ran as fast as I could to get away from this wild man. He kept right up with me but seemed not to be able to catch up, and so I kept running. Ahead I could see an old turkey feeder containing corn to bring in wild turkeys, and it was sitting probably 100 to 150 feet from the house because when I looked back I could still see the house.

"Just as I thought I'd never escape I got to the turkey feeder and the man stopped chasing me. I didn't stop though; I kept running all the way back to my parents' camp as fast as I could go.

"When I got there, I was out of breath and still frightened out of my wits, but when I told my parents and grandparents what had just happened, they just said I must have fallen asleep while fishing and just had a bad dream; either that or I was making up a story.

"Fortunately, my mother was more sympathetic, seeing how upset I was, and she said that she'd take me back and show me there was nothing to be frightened about. She held my hand as we walked back, and here and there we found the piles of bait I had dumped out before sitting down to fish.

"I pointed them out to mother as proof that at least this part of my story was true. Likewise, when we finally got up to the clearing, we could see the turkey feeder I had told them about. It was weird, but as we looked and looked around, we only saw a bare clearing. There was nothing else there at all; no house, no barn, no dog, and no doghouse!"

The traumatizing event, and her inability to produce any proof that it actually occurred, affected the little girl for years. Her mother knew she

Indian Attack on a Settler's cabin. (Painting attributed to Winslow Homer.) See Chapter 3, titled "War Whoop and Scalping Knife," for related tales.

continued to be traumatized by what had happened to her, and eventually she sent her to counseling sessions with a psychologist.

After several such sessions the doctor finally told the teenager that she should not feel that she was crazy. He agreed that she must have experienced something extraordinary and so she should not let others try to convince her otherwise.

The clearing where the cudgel-wielding man attacked the little girl is still there, and several years ago that same girl, now middle-aged and the mother of teenagers herself, took her children back to take a look. She had told them the story, and they wanted to see the spot for themselves.

They found the clearing again, and when they got there, they saw no house. Instead, there was an abandoned meat truck parked there and a fire pit where it looked like somebody had burned some old photos. Closer inspection of unburned pieces of the pictures that were still there revealed that the photos appeared to be wedding pictures from the 1920s.

The strange events still do not rest well with the woman who lived through them; she's convinced that there is an evil presence in the area where she had her strange experience. She thinks that's so, not only because of what happened to her there, but also because some years after her experience, her father and grandfather were sawing up wood here with their chain saws and her grandfather fell on his, cutting up his face badly enough that he had to be rushed to the emergency room.

Also, one year afterwards, she and her kids got carbon monoxide poisoning while staying at her dad's camp. It came from a refrigerator inside the camp. She almost died and her kids had to stay in oxygen tents in order to also recover.[1]

As I noted at the start of this chapter, this story is one of those that boggles the mind and makes us doubt what's true and what's not. It would certainly fit in nicely as one of Rod Serling's surreal *Twilight Zone* TV shows. On the other hand, the woman who told me this tale has no doubts as to what happened to her, and so it will remain just one more mysterious account from the dark woods, lonesome hollows, and foggy valleys of Pennsylvania's enchanted forests.

NOTE: Kohler Valley is not the only mountain fastness in Pennsylvania that can boast of its supernatural events. There is another such place in Clearfield County that deserves mention in this chapter due to the crazy occurrences that happened here at one time, placing it in a category of its own.

Up in the Moshannon State Forest, near Bucktail Boy Scout Council's Camp Mountain Run, and not far from the village of Penfield, there is a mountain road on Boone Mountain that leads to a remote "holler" that is known locally as Spook Hollow.

Those who have found it say it's hard to find, especially a second time, and they also say the hollow evokes a certain uneasiness in anyone who enters, mainly because of the eerie silence that prevails here. Nothing, not even a bird's song, seems to break the quietude, but that was not the case back in the 1920s when loud nightly noises echoed through the surrounding hills. These banging and clanging sounds always presaged a discovery the next morning that lumbering trucks and bulldozers belonging to the lumbering company working here had been vandalized by unseen hands.

Posting of guards did not prevent further destruction of equipment by the seemingly invisible forces, and after several instances where particularly

1. Lenna Mason (born 1961), interviewed September 11 and 12, 2013.

large lumber trucks were found in deformed shapes indicating they had been twisted like they were soft pretzels, the lumber company ceased its operations. See the author's tale titled "Man's Best Friend(ly ghost)" in *Volume IV* of this series for another ghostly tale from this same spot.

CHAPTER 14

FLYING THE MAIL

In 1987, when asked what the most amazing thing was that she had seen in her over ninety-two years of living, my grandmother Frazier hesitated not a bit when responding, "the airplane." It was a surprising answer, considering the other candidates from which she could have chosen.

In her lifetime, which began in the last years of the nineteenth century, and which ended in almost the final decade of the twentieth, she had seen the coming of the first electric light bulbs, television, and space flight, including the moon landing of 1969. And yet out of all those candidates it was the airplane that left the most lasting impression upon her. However, she was by no means highly impressionable, nor was she alone in her assessment; the early airplanes tended to catch peoples' attention, one way or another.[1]

One colorful example of how people reacted to the sight of the first airplanes was preserved in the oral historical annals of Penn Township, Centre County, where, during mankind's first decades of early flight, there lived, along Penns Creek and near the gap in the mountains called the Greenbriar Gap, a family named Auman.

Sade, and her husband Mode, were old pioneer stock, thoroughly Dutch, very old-fashioned, and used to eking a meager living from the land. It was, in fact, their isolation and backward way of life that kept them from being up-to-date on the latest news and current events, including the most recent developments in Europe during the first years of what was then called the Great War, but what we now refer to as World War I.

---

1. Mrs. Anna Jane Frazier (born 1895), interviewed 1987.

United States Airmail pilot Chandler. (Photo courtesy of Sherm Lutz.)

Apparently the Aumans were familiar with the airplane by then, but the war had left everyone a bit jittery. That could explain, along with the fact that planes in general were a rare sight in those times, why Sade reacted the way she did one day when a single plane appeared on the horizon.

"Mode, Mode, *hol die schrotflint,*" Mrs. Auman is reported to have cried, "*Hol die schrotflint,* the Germans are coming!" This all would have been said in Pennsylvania Dutch, and it's not known anymore today if

Mrs. Auman's husband ran to get his shotgun upon hearing his wife's calls, but the episode does preserve one example of those early days of flight and the many tales of human interest it produced.[2]

There are probably other stories like that of the Aumans' that could have been collected over the years, but among the most fascinating would have to be those that come down to us from the pilots who were among the first to fly the new "ships of the air."

And included in that elite coterie would be the men who risked their lives flying leftover, World War I, two-seater open-cockpit biplanes to deliver the mail when the United States started its air mail service in May of 1918.

They were often known by their nicknames, these adventurous young men who were as highly regarded as many sports figures and movie stars are today. Their popularity was such that even many years after they had hung up their wings "Hoppy" Hopson, "Ham" Lee, and "Charlie" Ames were still referred to in that way by the older people who felt privileged to have known them. However, certain pilots were more well-known and more popular than others, and it is their stories that have lasted the longest.

There were pilots, for example, like "Slim" Lewis, "who always managed to get through, even when the other pilots couldn't."[3] Once and a while though, he was delayed by reasons of his own doing. In those cases, he would slip a little camphor into his plane's gas tank so he "could lay over at his girlfriend's in Hecla Park while a mechanic at Bellefonte Airport would try to diagnose the craft's engine problems, finally fixing them by replacing the spark plugs."[4]

Then too there was "Wild Bill" Hobson, described by a fellow pilot who knew him as "smart, but a wild bastard with an airplane,"[5] Hobson's reputation was not unfounded, when it's recalled how he would sometimes hitch a night ride with another biplane pilot so he could visit his girlfriend. Hobson's bummed ride was not a trip for the faint-of-heart. "Wild Bill," recalled one man who knew him personally, would ride "out on the biplane's wing, hanging onto the fly wires!"[6]

---

2. Evelyn Breon (born 1918), recorded May 5, 1988.
3. Donald D. Jackson, "Slim Lewis Slept Here," *AIR AND SPACE Magazine*, October/November 1991.
4. Baptist Shank (born 1912), telephone interview, October 1997.
5. Trow Seebree (born 1904), telephone recordings September 1, 1991, and January 15, 1992.
6. Sherman Lutz (born 1903), recorded January 30, 1991.

United States Airmail pilot J. D. Hill. (Photo courtesy of Sherm Lutz.)

It's certainly clear that airmail flying was not a job for cowards. The secondhand de Havilland DH-4 army surplus biplanes, that were the workhorses of the Air Mail Service in its infant years, were just not reliable. The men who flew them often had to make emergency landings in farmers' fields or on any other open space they could find in order to avoid crashes.

"I made eight landings between Carrol, Iowa, and Chicago one time," recalled Harry Sievers who flew the old "Jennies," as they were referred to by the pilots, back in 1929. And he was not referring to airport landings since airfields were few and far between in those days. These were landings in open fields, and the grounded planes often drew the attention of people in the area.

"I had a problem I could fix real quick," explained Sievers, "and I could fix it and take off before anyone got out there. But I couldn't make a permanent repair. So I'd land, take the hood off and fix it, and be on my way before the farmer got out there!"[7]

On two other, more hazardous, occasions Sievers, who had bought himself a "WACO 10" aircraft back in 1925 and taught himself to fly, was carrying the mail between Cleveland and Pittsburgh and had to bail out twice. The first time his engine quit above a heavy fog layer, and the second time because of ice and wet snow on the wings.

"The airplane was like trying to fly a barn," was the way another old pilot described his flying experiences during those same years. "They didn't have the power when you needed it," went on Trow Seebree. "And they only would go fifty to sixty miles per hour at most!"[8]

Seebree proved to be a treasure house of tales from the old biplane days of the mail service, and according to him, the nickname the pilots chose for their planes, Jennies, came from their engine design number, JN4D. "If you talk real fast, he claimed, "it sounds like Jennie."[9]

Perhaps it was more like Jennifer D, and from there came Jenny, but it was Seebree's tales from the days of early aviation, especially those related to western and central Pennsylvania, that held an even greater fascination for us. They proved to be amazing links to that bygone age.

Born in 1904, Seebree became one of the Air Mail Service's first pilots after learning to fly in an old Canuck aircraft out in Flint, Michigan. Following that he then receiving professional training from the same man who had instructed Amelia Earhart.

"She knew how to run an airplane from A to B," claimed the former airmail pilot who had known the famous aviatrix personally, "but she couldn't get the goddamn thing off the ground a couple times except in a bucket, and she busted airplanes up two or three times," he chortled during a 1992 phone conversation.[10]

As far as his own expertise, Seebree commented that he "never had much faith in parachutes but had lots of opportunities to use them." In

7. Harry Sievers (born 1904), telephone recording January 10, 1992.
8. Seebree, Ibid.
9. Ibid.
10. Ibid.

that regard he had to admit that those who survived the flights, including himself, "were lucky; just plain lucky!" On the other hand, in looking back he also had to admit that it had been "lots of fun."

The old gentleman had logged many hours flying airmail biplanes between Pittsburgh and Cleveland back in the 1920s, and for years afterwards he was fond of relating several amusing anecdotes of his experiences on some of those trips. The tales always appealed to his avid listeners, but the one that must have always stuck in peoples' minds and caused them to chuckle whenever they thought about it, was the story of the night that Trow turned the lights out in Salem, Ohio.

"The bad part of the 1920s was that recession," was the way the biplane pilot would always start this hilarious story. "But everybody was getting electricity and all this stuff about the same time," he would continue. "You were supposed to fly where you could see the ground, and lots of times you'd get messed up. I had no instruments, and if you'd get on top of the clouds, you'd have a hell of a time finding anything at night! You had to have a very good memory! On nights with no moon, you could really see—see the lights of towns, and know exactly where they were, all the way. But when the moon comes out, it ruins your navigation!

"So we used to go over towns, like Salem, Ohio. And I had this fella with me named Howard Ross. He was my copilot, and this was his first trip, and as we were passing over Salem I said to him 'Hey, you oughta see what they do down there in Salem. We got a thing here where—' and I reached down underneath the dashboard, and I said, '—I can turn those lights off in that damn town down there!'

"And he said, 'You can do that?'

"And I said, 'I'll turn those lights off if you want me to!'

"And he said, 'You can't do that!' and I said 'I'll show you!'

"And I was watchin' the clock! At twelve midnight on the button, they'd turn all the lights off in Salem to save electricity, and so it got black as ink down there!

"He didn't say a word, but when we got to Pittsburgh he said, 'How in the hell did you find that switch that's doing all that stuff?'

"I said, 'Well, it's a secret. I'm not supposed to tell you about that.'

"I waited about a week before he went back with me again, and I told him what I had done. But when we got back over Salem that night, we

United States Airmail pilot Ward. Just one more example of those brave aviators who helped conquer the skies back in the infancy of the airline industry. (Photo courtesy of Sherm Lutz.)

still had to circle about twenty minutes so I could show him that the lights would go off by themselves without our help! He was ready to kill me!"[11]

One equally amusing story that the hardy pilot was fond of relating, was of the time in 1929 when his plane caused a man to fall off a boat in the middle of the Monongahela River above Pittsburgh. Told in his inimitable style, the anecdote proved to be as amusing as his previous one.

---

11. Ibid.

"Flying from Cleveland to Pittsburgh was probably the worst part of the United States for lousy weather and no lights, no radios, no nothin'!" noted Seebree. It was not an exaggeration if his statistics of "a pilot killed about every twenty-four days on that run" are true.

"We were takin' off at McKeesport, Pennsylvania, one night, headin' for Beaver Falls, and the weather was just awful," continued the former mail plane aviator. "But I took off, and my God, I didn't get fifty feet high, and, boom, right into a cloud!

"Now the airport and the whole area there is about 80 to 100 feet higher than the river, and they had these power lines going across the Monongahela, but I had to get down. I had a big hole in the clouds there in front of me, and I went down. Then I looked, and, oh my God, I almost hit a big power line goin' across the river! It was just before daylight, and I thought maybe I could get down there and circle someplace or do something.

"But I couldn't do anything, and I wasn't gonna hit any of those lines! So I went right down on top of the water. I thought 'if boats can get under those wires, then I can get under them too,' but there are twenty-two bridges between there and Butler, Pennsylvania.

"Anyway, I kept on goin', about ten to fifteen feet off the water all the way through, and I went under all those bridges! But up by a town called Aliquippa there was a boat with a guy standin' on top with a mop or something, and I had to pull up to get over the boat.

"He looked up just in time to see me coming, and he and the bucket and everything fell right overboard! I kept on goin'; I couldn't turn or do anything. I thought, I'm glad all he did was get wet!"[12]

Unfortunately, it was not the only time that airmail pilot Seebree got into trouble at that "same damn fool place."

"A week later we had the same," he recalled. "We had weather again, and I just couldn't make it! I couldn't get as far as Aliquippa, so I followed the railroad tracks on the east side of that river; in the Pittsburgh area there's all kinds of them. So, I thought 'Well, there's nothin' wrong with just landin' on the tracks! I was flying a Gates-Day Standard, and it had huge balloon tires with no axles. So I landed on the railroad tracks there at Aliquippa.

---

12. Ibid.

"And there was a guy came out there in the goddamn funniest old car you ever saw, and he said, 'You got trouble?'

"I [jokingly] said, 'Oh, no, no,' and he helped me get the darn thing off the railroad tracks. There was a railroad station there, and a place to park cars, so we pulled the plane over there. Then a guy in a big fancy Pearce-Arrow automobile comes up with his chauffeur and asked if there was anything he could do.

"I said, 'Yeah, I'd like to take this mail down to the Post Office, and I gotta call my boss; he'll probably fire me for doin' this!' (And he almost did, too!)

"The next morning, the wind was blowin' pretty good out of the north, and I was all set to go. I just went out there on the tracks and away we went. It wasn't too smooth, but the faster you went the better it was!"[13]

There was also another time when Seebree incurred the wrath of his boss. It happened one cold and rainy night about twenty miles from Beaver Falls, Pennsylvania. He was once again flying in another Gates-Day Standard aircraft, which he rated as "a fantastic airplane."

"If you had problems, you could land that thing in a field or anything," reminisced the old flyer. "You'd just tromp on the right brake as hard as you could when you hit the ground, and that locks the brake. That airplane would then twirl about one and a half times and then stop right there! I mean it wouldn't take up maybe a couple hundred feet of runway or field, or whatever you're in!

"One night right there in Beaver Falls, the doggone airplane got ice on it," explained Seebree. "When they do that, you never heard such a noise in your life! Those wings have wires on them which hold the wings up when you land and down when you're flyin'. They get coated with ice, and God almighty they make the doggonedest noise from the wind blowin' on them! Then all of a sudden it decides to quit flyin'! Down you go! And you better be quick when you're close to the ground—which I was!"

At that point Seebree was able to land in a farmer's field, where, when he looked up, he was alarmed to see "a whole row of trees right in front of me!" But when he slammed on the brake, he got a bit of a surprise.

"I almost went right over on my back," he recalled, fondly remembering those times. "I had a flyin' suit on with big flyin' boots, and I wasn't

13. Ibid.

First night mail plane arriving at Bellefonte Airport, July 1, 1925. Photo taken by Sherm Lutz, who was a barnstormer himself back in those days of first flight.

hurt or anything, but I was upside down and there was snow and mush on the ground. For some reason I unbuckled my seat belt, and my boot got caught on a dashboard lever that was used to prime the engine; pump gas into the cylinders. And my damn boot got caught on that damn thing!

"And I was hangin' by one foot, and I couldn't quite get up to unzip that damn boot! Finally, I got it sideways and got right side up and got out, but that's how I lost my boots out of that whole thing! It was cold and I was just about frozen, and in the distance, I could see a farmhouse, but nearby was the farmer's outhouse.

"Now I used to smoke quite a bit, so I had some cigarettes and matches in my flyin' suit pocket, and there were some rags in the plane. So, I opened up the gas tank and dipped the rags in there until they were full of gasoline. By then I was cold and numb, and so I threw the rags onto the side of the outhouse and touched a match to it! Boy, I got warm in a hurry!

"It wasn't long before the goddamn farmer and his wife and two kids come runnin'! They couldn't figure out what was goin' on, with an airplane upside down about a hundred feet from their house! But they were real nice.

"My boss was named Cliff Ball, he owned the airline (National Air Transport), and the farmer sent him a bill for a new outhouse! So, Cliff came to me and said, 'I didn't know you burned down an outhouse!'

"And I said, 'I did. I'm sorry, Cliff, I did. I was cold!'

"Well, it was $70.00 or something like that, and Cliff said, 'You buy him a new outhouse!'

"And I said, 'Okay', and I did!"[14]

There were times, however, when the audacious aviator had other chances to redeem himself. Many airmail pilots of that era had opportunities for alerting farmers that their houses, barns, or out-buildings were on fire, and Seebree did just that on several occasions.

"You'd see houses catch on fire, you know," he offered, "and burn at midnight or three o'clock in the morning. And you could see 'em! What you'd do is dive right over the damn thing and wake up the farmer! And my God, we'd wake 'em up too! And they'd get the animals out, that's the first thing they'd get; and then they'd try to put it out. But at least they were awake!"[15]

"Yeah, that's the kind of stuff we'd go through," concluded our colorful storyteller. He was eighty-eight years old at the time, and he was one of the most amazing links to the past I had encountered in, at that time, my twenty years of collecting the legends, folktales, and oral history of the Keystone State.

There were very few of his compatriots left, and they were passing away swiftly. Unfortunately, I did not have, nor did I take the time, to interview Hamilton ("Ham") Lee, who, I was told, was still alive and mentally sharp at 102 out in California. There were probably others as well, but other responsibilities and interests pulled me away from pursuing that field.

Today there are none of the early biplane airmail pilots around anymore, but they have not been forgotten. Museums preserve their pictures, and their children and other relatives remember their tales. Then too, traces of the legacy they left behind can also be found in out-of-the-way spots like the small memorial parklet on top of Nittany Mountain, just south of where the old Bellefonte Airport was located in Centre County.

Local Boy Scout Troop 20 of Centre Hall cleared a trail up to the site a number of years ago, and motorists traveling along Route 192 east of town will see the sign they erected to mark the trailhead about two miles outside town.

The James Cleveland Trail leads to the spot on top of the mountain where, on May 31st, 1931, airmail pilot James "Jimmy" Cleveland became

---

14. Ibid.
15. Ibid.

the last fatality of the pilots who had flown into the old Bellefonte Airfield over the years. A hike up to the sacred spot is a rocky one, but those who make it to the top will see the stone monument erected to commemorate the crash site along with pieces of wreckage from the plane itself.

An historical marker also marks the site of the old Bellefonte Airport, now the site of the Bellefonte Area Senior High School, but most passing motorists probably don't even notice the sign as they whiz by today. However, even the pilots themselves didn't appreciate the site all that much.

"It was a must stop," said Trow Seebree, "but not a good place to stop, right there in the middle of a little valley and high hills all around it."

Bellefonte, it turns out, was a refueling stop. The old DH's had "great big engines that burned a lot of fuel, and they couldn't go very fast," recalled pilot Seebree, who had himself flown into Bellefonte when flying the mail. "They could go from Newark to Bellefonte, but they had to land in Bellefonte because they didn't have enough gas to take 'em to Cleveland. And they bumped into those hills all the time," said the old pilot.

In fact, it was the many crashes through here that earned the area the bleak names of "Hell Stretch" and "Graveyard Run." The strong updrafts from the mountain peaks, the planes' feeble engines, and nonexistent or primitive instrumentation all contributed to the dangers of the job. "About every time you left the ground you were a potential one [crash victim]"[16] is the way Trow Seebree summed it up, and it is to him and his fellow flyers that this chapter is most respectfully dedicated.

---

16. Seebree, Ibid.

ACKNOWLEDGEMENTS

To those who created, by the very lives they lived, the human-interest tales and stirring episodes that have colored Pennsylvania's mountains and valleys with charm, mystery, and a seemingly endless source of intriguing episodes of days gone by.

And to those who have preserved those Pennsylvania episodes: "He who seeks out and preserves the local traditions of a region and casts them into forms of beauty is building a monument to himself more lasting than stone or metal."

From a letter, dated November 1, 1916, sent to Henry W. Shoemaker by Fred Lewis Pattee (as found on page 90 of the book by Simon Bronner titled *Popularizing Pennsylvania*).

BIBLIOGRAPHY

Beers, J. H. and Co., *Commemorative Biographical Record of Southwestern Pennsylvania, Including the Counties of Centre, Clinton, Union, and Snyder*, Chicago, 1898.

———, *History of Mckean, Elk, Cameron, and Potter Counties Pennsylvania*, Chicago, 1890.

Benton, William, publisher, *Encyclopedia Britannica, 15th Edition*, Chicago, Encyclopedia Brittanica, Inc., 1975.

Blackman, Emily C., *History of Susquehanna County, Pennsylvania*, Philadelphia, Claxton, Remsen and Haffelfinger, 1873.

Boucher, John N., *History of Westmoreland County, Pennsylvania*, NY, The Lewis Publishing Company, 1906.

Brendle, Thomas R. and William S. Troxell, "Pennsylvania German Folk Tales, Legends, Once-upon-a-time Stories, Maxims, and Sayings," *Proceedings of the Pennsylvania German Society—Volume L*, Norristown, PA, Pennsylvania German Society, 1944.

Brooks, J. A., *Britain's Haunted Heritage*, Jarrold Publishing, Norwich, England, 1990.

———, *Ghosts and Legends of Wales*, Jarrold Publishing, Norwich, England, 1987.

Carmer, Carl, *The Susquehanna*, Rinehart and Co., NY, 1955.

Cornplanter, Jesse J., *Legends of the Longhouse*, Port Washington, NY, Ira J. Friedman, 1963.

Craft, Reverend David, *History of Bradford County, Pennsylvania*, Philadelphia, L. H. Everts, 1878.

Day, Sherman, *Historical Collections of the State of Pennsylvania*, Port Washington, NY, Ira J. Friedman, 1843.

Dubbs, Paul M., *Where-to-go and Place Names of Centre County*, State College, PA, Nittany Printing and Publishing, 1961.

Elliott, Ella Zerbey, *Blue Book of Schuylkill County*, Pottsville, PA, The Pottsville Press, 1916.

Faris, John T., *Seeing Pennsylvania*, Philadelphia, J. B. Lippincott, 1919.

Fiske, John, *Myths and Myth-makers (Old Tales and Superstitions Interpreted by Comparative Mythology)*, Boston, Houghton Mifflin and Co., 1893.

Fletcher, Stevenson W., *Pennsylvania Agriculture & Country Life, 1640-1840*, Harrisburg, PA, Historical and Museum Commission, 1971.

Hardwick, Charles, *Traditions, Superstitions, and Folk-lore, (Chiefly Lancashire and the North of England)*, Manchester, England, A. Ireland & Co., 1872.

Heverly, Clement F., *History and Geography of Bradford County, Pennsylvania*, Towanda, PA, Bradford County Historical Society, 1926.

———, *Pioneer and Patriot Families of Bradford County, Pennsylvania*, Towanda, PA, Bradford Star Printing, 1913-1915.

Hunt, Robert, *Popular Romances of the West of England, Or The Drolls, Traditions, and Superstitions of Old Cornwall*, Bronx, NY, R. B. Blom Inc., 1916.

Ingram, John H., *The Haunted Homes and Family Traditions of Great Britain*, London, Reeves and Turner Co., 1905.

Linn, John Blair, *History of Centre and Clinton Counties, Pennsylvania*, Philadelphia, Louis H. Everts Co., 1883.

———, *Annals of Buffalo Valley, Pennsylvania 1755-1855*, Harrisburg, PA, Lane S. Hart, Printer and Binder, 1877.

Longfellow, Henry W., *The Poetical Works of Henry Wadsworth Longfellow*, Boston, MA, James R. Osgood and Co., 1877.

Lyman, Robert R., *Amazing Indeed (Strange Events in the Black Forest—Volume 2)*, Coudersport, PA, The Potter Enterprise, 1973.

McCloy, James F. and Ray Miller Jr., *The Jersey Devil*, Wallingford, PA, Mid Atlantic Press, 1976.

Magargel, Mytrle, *History of Pleasant Gap*, Centre Daily Times Publications, 1936.

———, *The History of Rock*, State College, Pennsylvania, Centre Daily Times Publications, 1940.

Maple, Eric, *Origins: Superstitions and their Meanings*, Reader's Digest, 1978.

Meginness, John F., *Otzinachson, A History of the West Branch Valley*, Williamsport, PA, Gazette Printing House, 1889.

———, *History of Lycoming County Pennsylvania*, Chicago, Brown, Runk, and Co., 1892.

Montgomery, Thomas L., editor, *Frontier Forts of Pennsylvania*, Harrisburg, PA, Pennsylvania Historical Commission, 1916.

Parkman, Francis, *History of the Conspiracy of Pontiac*, New York, The Macmillan Company, 1929.

Peck, George, D. D., *Wyoming; Its History, Stirring Incidents, and Romantic Adventures*, New York, Harper and Brothers, 1858.

Rondthaler, Reverend Edward, *Life of John Heckewelder*, Philadelphia, Townsend Ward, 1847.

Rosenberger, Homer Tope, *Mountain Folks (Fragments of Central Pennsylvania Lore)*, Lock Haven, PA, Annie Halenbake Ross Library, 1974.

Sassaman, Grant N., ed., *Pennsylvania, A Guide to the Keystone State*, Pennsylvania Writers' Project, New York, Oxford University Press, 1940.

Sipe, C. Hale, *The Indian Chiefs of Pennsylvania*, Butler, PA, Ziegler Printing Co., 1927.

———, *The Indian Wars of Pennsylvania*, Harrisburg, The Telegraph Press, 1931.

Skinner, Charles M., *Myths and Legends of Our Own Land*, Philadelphia, J. B. Lippincott, 1896.

Tantaquidgeon, Gladys, *Folk Medicine of the Delaware*, Harrisburg, Pennsylvania Historical Commission, 1972.

Tome, Phillip, *Pioneer Life, or Thirty Years a Hunter*, Baltimore, Gateway Press, 1989, reprint of the 1854 edition.

Tylor, Sir Edward B., *Primitive Culture: Researches into the Development of Mythology, Philosophy, Religion, Language, Art, and Custom, Volume I*, London, John Murray & Co., 1903.

Wallace, Paul A. W., *Indians in Pennsylvania*, Harrisburg, Pennsylvania Historical Commission, 1970.

Warner, Beers & Co., *History of Franklin County Pennsylvania*, Chicago, 1887.

Williams, Harry M., *The Story of Scotia*, State College, PA, Centre County Historical Society, 1992.

ABOUT THE AUTHOR

JEFFREY R. FRAZIER was born and raised in Centre Hall, Centre County, where he says he grew up in a "Tom Sawyer sort of way," later graduating with a BS from Penn State in 1967, and then an MBA from Rider University in New Jersey in 1978.

Some of the fondest memories of his boyhood include explorations of out-of-the-way spots in the mountains and hearing accounts of the legends that seem to cling to them. Then, beginning in 1970, he began collecting those same kind of anecdotes from all over the state; ranging from the Blue Mountains of Berks and Lehigh Counties, the South Mountains of Adams County, the "Black Forest" area of Potter and Tioga Counties, the Alleghenies of Clearfield and Blair Counties, and the other counties in the middle. He has compiled his vast collection of tales into an eight-volume series titled *Pennsylvania Fireside Tales*. This volume is a continuation of his work, written in a format that the average reader can enjoy, especially for those who love the green valleys and cloud-covered mountain peaks of Pennsylvania as much as he does.